P9-DDX-441

LEADERS *of* LEARNING

{ How District, School, and Classroom Leaders Improve Student Achievement }

RICHARD DUFOUR
ROBERT J. MARZANO

Solution Tree | Press

a division of

Solution Tree

Copyright © 2011 by Solution Tree Press

All rights reserved, including the right of reproduction of this book in whole or in part in any form.

555 North Morton Street

Bloomington, IN 47404

800.733.6786 (toll free) / 812.336.7700

FAX: 812.336.7790

email: info@solution-tree.com

solution-tree.com

Printed in the United States of America

15 14 13 12   4 5

Library of Congress Cataloging-in-Publication Data

DuFour, Richard.

    Leaders of learning : how district, school, and classroom leaders improve student achievement / Richard DuFour, Robert J. Marzano.

        p. cm.

    Includes bibliographical references and index.

    ISBN 978-1-935542-66-7 (perfect bound) -- ISBN 978-1-935542-67-4 (library edition) 1. Educational leadership. 2. School improvement programs. 3. Academic achievement. I. Marzano, Robert J. II. Title.

    LB2805.D86 2012

    371.2'011--dc22

                    2011013060

Solution Tree

Jeffrey C. Jones, CEO & President

Solution Tree Press

President: Douglas M. Rife

Publisher: Robert D. Clouse

Vice President of Production: Gretchen Knapp

Managing Production Editor: Caroline Wise

Senior Production Editor: Suzanne Kraszewski

Proofreader: Rachel Rosolina

Cover Designer: Jenn Taylor

Text Designer: Orlando Angel

What Researchers Are Saying About
Leaders of Learning

"Finally we have a book that gives strategic thinkers the blueprint for implementing PLCs up and down the levels of authority and levels of influence in a whole school system. Sustainable change requires pressing the key levers of influence at the same time and knowing how they interact with one another. This book gives crystal clarity to what PLCs really are and how to get them; but on the way, it becomes a brilliant tract and hands-on guide for systemic change and the subtleties of leadership."

—Jonathon Saphier, Founder and Chairman Emeritus of Teachers21,
Founder and President of Research for Better Teaching

"Many of us advocating the need for a 21st century education model have focused primarily on what capabilities students need to have to be effective 21st century citizens and workers. We have not focused adequately on the how. We knew intuitively that we needed new approaches and new environments and that PLCs needed to be part of the solution. DuFour and Marzano's critical new book lays out the path quite clearly. What do 21st century learning environments need to look like? What roles and responsibilities do teachers, principals, and administrators have in this new environment? What are the new ground rules for effective collaborative work? They address these essential questions with great alacrity, and therefore *Leaders of Learning* will become one of the 'must have' volumes of the new 21st century education literature."

—Ken Kay, CEO, EdLeader21

"Don't ask how to make a difference in classrooms—this book will show you the most effective ways to make a difference in classrooms. The authors interpret ample research studies to show how classroom and school leaders can come together to not only know whether they are making a difference, but also to optimise the most successful strategies that lead to the most powerful changes."

—John Hattie, Professor of Education,
University of Auckland, New Zealand

"This is a really great book that not only explains leadership well but also explains very practically how everyone in a school community can become accomplished in leadership."
—Sir Michael Barber, Head of McKinsey's Global Education Practice and Chair of the Pakistan Education Taskforce; Former Chief Adviser on Delivery to the British Prime Minister, Tony Blair

"DuFour and Marzano team up to give us a definition of the kind of leadership that can ultimately lead to the closing of America's achievement gap. Leadership is not an individual act but, rather, a team effort. Don't look for superman at the top of the organizational chart—look at leaders from the boardroom to the classroom to make the difference in the lives of our children. A must-read."
—Dan Domenech, Executive Director, American Association of School Administrators

What District Leaders Are Saying About *Leaders of Learning*

"Inspiring, insightful, practical, and results based—DuFour and Marzano have taken their research and experience and coupled them in such a way as to not only inform, but also inspire school leaders. Any district in the country willing to implement the strategies in this book will see substantial improvement."
—Tom Trigg, Superintendent of Schools, Blue Valley Schools, Overland Park, Kansas; 2011 Finalist for National Superintendent of the Year

"*Leaders of Learning* is a must-read for teachers and leaders who are passionate about improving schools where students are at the heart of every instructional decision and staff are provided with the tools they need to be effective. The authors combine their years of proven practice, research, and practical know-how to develop a framework that can be used by schools and districts alike to ensure that every student is provided with the supports he or she needs to learn at a high level. This book outlines a clear and comprehensive approach to school improvement that challenges educators to create authentic PLCs where staff members collaborate and continuously reflect upon and improve their teaching practices to guarantee that each student is taught by a winning team of professional educators. DuFour and Marzano have hit a grand slam in their latest work!"

—Ed Rafferty, Superintendent, Schaumburg Community
Consolidated School District 54, Schaumburg, Illinois;
2010 Illinois Superintendent of the Year

"*Leaders of Learning* sends a powerful, clear message to public educators regarding our collective moral imperative to continue to improve. It is a resounding call to action. DuFour and Marzano identify our collective responsibilities at the classroom, school, and district level to share leadership, apply research-proven effective strategies to our daily work, and take action to meet students' diverse learning needs. DuFour and Marzano identify missteps we can avoid and give clear direction about what we need to do to realize high levels of success in public education."

—Mary Alice Heuschel, Superintendent,
Renton School District, Renton, Washington;
2011 Finalist for National Superintendent of the Year

"Today, the job of leadership in our schools has changed dramatically; from the boardroom to the classroom, we must all understand our roles as leaders of learning. Marzano and DuFour have done a masterful job of describing the collaborative environments we must build to support the learning needs of every child and the leadership roles that must be filled to successfully build those collaborative cultures focused on student learning. *Leaders of Learning* charts the course from empowerment and capacity building, through guaranteed and viable curriculum and measuring learning, to developing supports for those who struggle on the way. This book clearly defines the path we all must walk if we are to realize the moral imperative of every child learning."

—Marcus Johnson, Superintendent, Sanger Unified School District,
Fresno County, California; 2011 National Superintendent of the Year

What School Leaders and Teachers Are Saying About *Leaders of Learning*

"Although top thinkers in the education reform movement have stressed the need to develop teachers as leaders, the challenge has always been defining exactly what teacher leadership looks like in action. That's what makes *Leaders of Learning* such an important read. Building on Rick's extensive experience with professional learning communities and Bob's understanding of what works in schools, *Leaders of Learning* details a collection of practical action steps—from developing a guaranteed and viable curriculum to systematically monitoring student learning—that teachers interested in leading can begin taking immediately. As a full-time classroom teacher, I'm thankful to finally have a practical guide detailing the kinds of significant contributions I can make in my classroom, on my learning team, and across our school."

—Bill Ferriter, Founding Member and Senior Fellow
of the Teacher Leadership Network

"Brilliant book on district, site, and teacher leadership in a PLC. The authors bring into perfect clarity the critical roles of leadership at all levels of the school organization with a combination of practical approaches based on solid research. "

—Garrick Peterson, Principal, Lakeridge Junior High School, Orem, Utah

"As a teacher at Adlai Stevenson High School, I saw the power of the PLC process, a process that made it possible for me to share with colleagues and learn from them. *Leaders of Learning* presents a compelling case for establishing the PLC process in every district, school, and classroom. It provides solid examples that ground this book in the reality of everyday teacher-leaders; articulates what good teaching looks and feels like; and provides practical strategies and resources. Dan Rather once said that the best teachers take students to higher levels of learning by 'sometimes poking you with a sharp stick called "truth."' This book brings you to the next level by gently, but emphatically, prodding you with research-based truth."

—Tom Koenigsberger, Former High School Teacher,
Adlai E. Stevenson High School, Lincolnshire, Illinois

To Becky
—Rick DuFour

To the future: Cecilia, Aida, Jacob, Taya, and Jagger
—Bob Marzano

Acknowledgments

It has been my great pleasure and privilege to include some of the most influential educational thinkers in North America as colleagues. My conversations and correspondence with Michael Fullan, Doug Reeves, Rick Stiggins, Larry Lezotte, Jon Saphier, Mike Schmoker, and Dennis Sparks have shaped and sharpened my own thinking. I am grateful for the support they have given me and for the great grace with which they offer it. The opportunity to coauthor this book with Bob Marzano, someone whose work I have so admired and respected, is an enormous thrill for me.

I am also deeply indebted to the great practitioners with whom I have worked. There are far too many to mention, but I would be remiss if I didn't acknowledge my debt to the faculty and staff of Adlai Stevenson High School and to the many colleagues who are helping implement the professional learning community process in schools across the world. One of those colleagues, Bob Eaker, has been my best friend and collaborator for over thirty years. I have benefitted tremendously from the wisdom and insights he brings to our partnership. His friendship is a gift that keeps on giving.

Jeff Jones has been not only my publisher, but also a passionate advocate for my work. His vision and energy have transformed a small publishing company into one of the leading providers of quality professional development in North America. I treasure my personal and professional relationship with this extraordinary man. Solution Tree's Robb Clouse and Gretchen Knapp were instrumental in arranging for the collaboration that led to this book. Suzanne Kraszewski has edited and improved every book I have written.

Finally, it is impossible to express adequately how the support and love of Becky Burnette DuFour has impacted and enriched my thinking, my work, and my life. She inspires me on a daily basis.

—Richard DuFour

I must start by acknowledging those professional colleagues who have dramatically expanded my understanding of K–12 education. At the top of the list is probably Rick DuFour himself. A few years ago I told Rick that the PLC movement as crafted by him, Bob Eaker, and Becky DuFour was probably the most influential movement with regards to actually changing practices in schools I had ever seen. That sentiment is still true for me. I am greatly honored to have the chance to write this book with him. Others to whom I owe a debt of gratitude include (in no particular order): Doug Reeves, Tom Guskey, Rick Stiggins, Mike Schmoker, Jay McTighe, Grant Wiggins, Carol Ann Tomlinson, Tim Waters, Diane Paynter, and Debra Pickering.

I must acknowledge Jeff Jones who is my partner in Marzano Research Laboratory, which is a dream come true for me. Without Jeff, that dream would have never been realized.

Finally, and most importantly, I must recognize my wife of thirty years, Jana. Being married to a man whose idea of fun is writing a book probably gets old very quickly. Not only has Jana supported those efforts, but she has been a constant source of inspiration. She is my partner, my lover, and my muse.

—Robert J. Marzano

Table of Contents

About the Authors

Richard DuFour, EdD, was a public school educator for thirty-four years, serving as a teacher, principal, and superintendent. He is the only educator in Illinois to receive the state's Distinguished Educator award as a principal and Award of Excellence as a superintendent. He was presented the Distinguished Scholar Practitioner Award from the University of Illinois and the Distinguished Service Award from the National Staff Development Council.

Dr. DuFour is the author of twenty books and videos and over ninety professional articles. He is one of the nation's leading authorities on implementation of the Professional Learning Community process and consults with school districts, state departments, and professional organizations throughout the world on strategies for improving schools.

Robert J. Marzano, PhD, is cofounder and CEO of Marzano Research Laboratory in Englewood, Colorado. A leading researcher in education, he is a speaker, trainer, and author of more than 30 books and 150 articles on topics such as instruction, assessment, writing and implementing standards, cognition, effective leadership, and school intervention. His books include *Designing & Teaching Learning Goals & Objectives, District Leadership That Works, Formative Assessment & Standards-Based Grading, On Excellence in Teaching,*

and *The Art and Science of Teaching.* His practical translations of the most current research and theory into classroom strategies are internationally known and widely practiced by both teachers and administrators.

Dr. Marzano received a bachelor's degree from Iona College in New York, a master's degree from Seattle University, and a doctorate from the University of Washington.

To learn more about Richard DuFour's work, please visit www.allthingsplc.info.

To learn more about Robert Marzano's work, please visit www.marzanoresearch.com, or follow robertjmarzano on Twitter.

To book Dr. DuFour or Dr. Marzano for professional development, contact pd@solution-tree.com.

Introduction

Viewing leadership as a group activity linked to
practice rather than just an individual activity linked to
a person helps match the expertise we have in a school
with the problems and situations we face.

—Thomas Sergiovanni

Every person who enters the field of education has both an opportunity and an obligation to be a leader. That is the premise of this book, and it flies in the face of traditional assumptions about leadership in the United States.

Americans are prone to think of leadership as an individual activity linked to a position. If aliens were to ask, "Take me to your leader," most people would look to the top of the organizational chart. Furthermore, Americans often think the ability to lead is reserved for a heroic few, those individuals who save us from ourselves by making up for our deficiencies.

We have heard this story over and over again: the brilliant entrepreneurial leader who saves the company from ruin (think Jack Welch), the military figure whose personal genius and charisma lead to victory (think George Patton), the athlete who saves us from defeat through his personal gifts and force of will (think Michael Jordan), or the principal who single-handedly turns a school around (think Joe Clark in the movie *Lean on Me*). Leaders solve our problems because they not only have the answer—they *are* the answer.

It is time to let go of the myth of the charismatic individual leader who has it all figured out. No single person can unilaterally bring about substantive change in an organization. Two researchers who have made the study of leadership their life's work put it this way:

> In the thousands of cases we've studied, we've yet to encounter a single example of extraordinary achievement that didn't involve the active participation and support of many people. We've yet to find a single instance in which one talented person—leader or individual contributor—accounted for most, let alone 100 percent, of the success. Throughout the years, leaders from all professions, from all economic sectors, and from around the globe continue to tell us, "You can't do it alone." Leadership is not a solo act; it's a team performance. . . . The winning strategies will be based upon the "we" not "I" philosophy. Collaboration is a social imperative. Without it people can't get extraordinary things done in organizations. (Kouzes & Posner, 2003, p. 22)

Effective leaders recognize that they cannot accomplish great things alone. They also recognize that the ability to lead is not the private reserve of a few extraordinary people or those in particular positions of authority. They acknowledge that leadership capacity is "broadly distributed in the population and is accessible to anyone who has passion and purpose to change things as they are" (Kouzes & Posner, 2010, p. 5).

In this book, we argue that no single person has all the knowledge, skills, and talent to lead a district, improve a school, or meet all the needs of every child in his or her classroom. We assert that it will take a collaborative effort and widely dispersed leadership to meet the challenges confronting our schools, and we stress that virtually everyone who has elected to enter the field of education has the potential to lead.

Those who believe that leadership is determined by the organizational chart may be puzzled by the premise that teachers should be considered leaders. That premise, however, is fundamental to this book. As John Gardner (1993) wrote, "Every great leader is clearly teaching and every great teacher is leading" (p. 18). In some of his workshops, Rick asks half of the group to think of the very best leader they have known. He asks the other half to think of the very best teacher they have known. Each group then lists the qualities or characteristics of that leader or teacher. Inevitably, the lists are the same. Both groups describe someone "who inspired me," "who believed in me," "who challenged me to accomplish more than I thought I could," "who had a contagious passion for the work."

Leadership is ultimately about the ability to influence others. Teachers, like all leaders, seek results that cannot possibly be achieved solely by their own efforts. They must convince others (in their case, students) to act in ways that produce the intended results. As a longitudinal study of effective teaching concluded:

> Our most effective teachers show that great teaching is *leadership*. . . . In every highly effective classroom, we find a teacher who, like any great leader, rallies team members (in this case, students and their families) around an ambitious vision of success. We find a teacher who plans purposefully and executes effectively to make sure students reach that vision, even as that teacher also continues to learn and improve. (Farr, 2010, p. 30)

When Kouzes and Posner (2010) asked thousands of people who had the greatest influence on their lives, teachers were second only to parents. They wrote, "If you're in a role that brings you into contact with young people on a regular basis—say a parent, teacher, coach, or counselor—keep this observation in mind. Someone is looking to you right now for leadership" (p. 10). So this book will not only talk about district, principal, and team leadership, it will also address how individual teachers can be most effective in leading their students by learning with their colleagues how to implement the most promising pedagogy in their classrooms.

Although this is our first book together, we have admired each other's work for years as we have been cotravelers on the journey to help educators improve their schools. As Rick has focused on bringing the professional learning community (PLC) process to life in schools, he has relied heavily on Bob's vast research on effective teaching and effective leadership. Bob has come to the conclusion that the best environment for great teaching and leading is a powerful PLC. So it made sense to us to combine our passions into one book that could articulate how effective leaders foster continuous improvement at the district, school, and classroom levels.

We have learned a great deal from one another as we engaged in this collaborative effort to provide a helpful resource to educators. We hope that we have met the goal. More importantly, we hope that regardless of your position, you will embrace your opportunity to lead—to act in ways that inspire others to dream more, learn more, do more, and become more.

CHAPTER 1

School Improvement Means People Improvement

Public schools are being asked to do more with less for
an increasingly more needy clientele.

—Larry Lezotte

Contemporary American educators confront the most daunting
challenge in the history of public schooling in the United States:
they are called upon to raise academic standards to the highest
level in history with common core standards that are so rigorous
and include such challenging cognitive demands that they align
with the highest international benchmarks (National Governors
Association, Chief Council of State School Officials, & Achieve, Inc.,
2008). Furthermore, schools are to bring *every* student to these dramatically higher standards of academic achievement. No generation of educators in the history of the United States has ever been
asked to do so much for so many.

Teachers and administrators are expected to meet these unprecedented standards while serving an increasing number of students
who historically have struggled to find success in traditional
schools. Huge racial gaps exist in the United States in graduation
rates, test scores, and advanced proficiency. According to a study
by the McKinsey Group, black and Latino students are, on average, two to three years behind white students of the same age in
academic achievement, and their high school graduation rates

are 20 percent lower than the rate of white students (Alliance for Excellent Education, 2008). The percentage of black and Latino students is increasing in the United States, and by 2023 the nation's students will be a minority majority. As the McKinsey study concluded, "As a greater proportion of blacks and Latinos enter the student population in the United States, the racial achievement gap, if not addressed, will almost certainly act as a drag on overall US educational and economic performance in the years ahead" (p. 11).

Another enormous gap in educational attainment in the United States is based on the socioeconomic status of students. Students eligible for free and reduced lunch "are roughly two years of learning behind the average better-off student of the same age" (McKinsey & Company, 2009, p. 12). This gap persists beyond the K–12 system. A child growing up in a family earning $90,000 annually has a one in two chance of earning a bachelor's degree by the age of twenty-four, but a child from a family earning less than $35,000 has only a one in seventeen chance of earning that degree (Brooks, 2005). As the National Center for Public Policy and Education (2005) warns, if the educational gaps remain as they are, "the proportion of workers with high school diplomas and college degrees will decrease and the personal income of Americans will decline over the next 15 years" (p. 1).

No educational system in the history of the world has ever accomplished what American educators are now called upon to do. To make their challenge even more formidable, the resources available to support their efforts are being slashed. The *New York Times* (Lewin & Dillion, 2010) reported, "The 2010–11 school year is shaping up as one of the most austere in the last half century." The economic downturn, devaluation of real estate, and plunging state revenues have had a devastating effect on school revenues, leading to cuts in educational expenditures throughout the United States. The Draconian cuts to school budgets and massive dismissal of school personnel led Secretary of Education Arne Duncan to warn that the nation was flirting with "educational catastrophe." Districts warn of deeper teacher cuts.

These are the brutal facts confronting the men and women in our schools—demands that they raise academic standards to levels that were unimaginable to previous generations of educators, that they ensure *every* child achieves these new standards and eliminate achievement gaps that have persisted throughout American history, and that they attain this unprecedented accomplishment with dwindling resources. Let's consider how they might respond to this reality.

Denial

A legitimate case can be made that American schools are better than ever. Consider the following:

- Between 1960 and 2000 the percentage of Americans twenty-five years of age or older with a high school diploma almost doubled from 41 percent to 80 percent (United States Census Bureau, 2010).

- More students are opting for the most rigorous curriculum their high schools have to offer (National Assessment of Educational Progress, 2007). The College Board (2010) reported that more students are writing advanced placement (AP) exams, a higher percentage are earning honor scores, minority and low-income students are participating in greater numbers, and "across the nation, educators and policy makers are helping a wider segment of the United States' population experience success in AP" (p. 2).

- Between 1987 and 2006, the average SAT score in both the verbal and mathematics section of the exam increased for every one of the six subgroups identified by the College Board. The scores in writing have increased for all subgroups since 1996 when the test was initiated (Korbin, Sathy, & Shaw, 2007).

- The percentage of the public giving their local schools
  the grade of A or B has increased significantly in the
  past twenty-five years. In 2009, 51 percent of Americans
  assigned the schools in their community the grade of A or
  B, equaling the highest percentage since the poll was begun
  in 1969. In that same poll, almost 75 percent of parents
  with children in school gave the school their oldest child
  attended the grade of A or B, the highest mark in the history of the poll (Bushaw & McNee, 2009).

In the face of this happy news, educators may be content to insist
that all is well. To do so, however, obscures some chilling realities
regarding the U.S. educational system.

- Until the final decades of the 20th century, the United
  States had the best high school graduation rate in the
  world. By 2006 it had slipped to eighteenth out of twenty-
  six industrialized countries (Organisation for Economic
  Co-operation and Development, 2010).

- As recently as 1995, the United States was tied for first in
  the proportion of young adults with a college degree, but by
  2000 it had slipped to ninth, and by 2006 to fourteenth—
  falling below the average of the countries that comprise the
  Organisation for Economic Co-operation and Development
  (OECD, 2010).

- The United States has the second-highest college dropout
  rate among twenty-seven countries (National Governors
  Association et al., 2008).

- American students do not fare well on international
  exams, and the longer they are in school, the worse their
  performance gets. The results on a recent Programme for
  International Student Assessment (PISA) revealed that out
  of thirty industrialized countries, American fifteen-year-
  olds ranked twenty-fifth in math, twenty-first in science,

fifteenth in reading, and twenty-fourth in problem solving (National Governor's Association et al., 2008).

- The relatively low performance does not apply solely to students demonstrating proficiency. The United States has among the smallest percentage of its students scoring at the highest proficiency in math. Korea, Switzerland, Belgium, Finland, and the Czech Republic have five times the proportion of top performers as the United States (McKinsey & Company, 2009).

- More than one-third of American high school graduates who enter college are required to take remedial courses at a cost of over $2 billion annually. Nearly four of every five of those students had a high school grade point average of 3.0 or higher. Furthermore, the chances of earning a degree are significantly diminished for college students who require remediation. Only 12 percent of the students enrolled in remedial college reading courses eventually earn a degree (Strong American Schools, 2008).

A system that has 30 percent of its students drop out of high school, that has one-third of its graduates who enter higher education requiring remediation, that has one of the highest college dropout rates in the world, that contributes to enormous gaps in achievement for minority and poor students, and that has seen its relative success in educating its population plummet compared to other nations cannot assume the position that all is well. Denying the existence of a problem does not serve either the national interest or the individual students schools are intended to serve.

The large number of students who drop out of school because of their inability to find success there represents a continuing drain on the U.S. economy. The resulting underutilization of human capital has been described as the "equivalent of a permanent deep recession in terms of the gap between actual and potential output of the economy" (McKinsey & Company, 2009, p. 18). Closing that gap between minority and white students, for example, would contribute an estimated $500 billion to the gross domestic product each year.

But even if there were no national imperative to improve the education of our students, there is a moral imperative. Throughout most of U.S. history, education was merely one path to the American dream. High school dropouts had ready access to the middle class because of relatively high-paying jobs in manufacturing, construction, and mining. By 1998, however, the percentage of workers in these goods-producing industries had dropped to 17 percent, a decline that is projected to continue through 2018 when it will reach 12.9 percent because *these industries are projected "to show virtually no growth" in jobs* (Bureau of Labor Statistics, 2009; emphasis added).

The service industry, which accounted for only 15 percent of American jobs in 1960, now constitutes over 70 percent of those jobs. Virtually all of the 15 million new jobs projected to be created between 2008 and 2018 are in the service industry, and approximately half of them will require a postsecondary degree. Fourteen of the fastest growing job classifications have a bachelor's degree or higher as the most significant source of postsecondary education or training for entry to the position. Increasingly, education is becoming a prerequisite for access to the American dream (Bureau of Labor Statistics, 2009).

The high school dropout rate adversely impacts not only the national economy but also the students themselves. Three out of every ten students in America's public schools still fail to finish high school with a diploma. That amounts to 1.3 million students lost from the 9–12 pipeline every year—the equivalent of 7,150 students every school day or approximately one student every twenty-five seconds (Swanson, 2009). The implications for these students are dire. We can predict that those dropouts:

- Are likely to earn only thirty-six cents for every dollar a college graduate earns and sixty-seven cents for every dollar earned by a high school graduate (United States Census Bureau, 2009)

- Will be more prone to ill health and will live a shorter life; a college graduate is projected to live ten years longer than a student who drops out of school at sixteen (Kolata, 2007)

- Will be less employable in a volatile job market (Bureau of Labor Statistics, 2009)

- Will be five to eight times more likely to be incarcerated than a college graduate (McKinsey & Company, 2009)

When educators impact not only the quality of life of their students, but also the duration of their students' lives, they are certainly serving a moral purpose that flies in the face of complacency. Every educator confronts a moral imperative to seek the most promising strategies for helping every student achieve at high levels.

Failed Strategies

The idea of improving schools is not new. The history of education in the United States in the 20th century is essentially the history of the effort to reform schools. The publication of *A Nation at Risk* in 1983 by the National Commission on Excellence in Education was certainly a landmark in that effort. The Commission warned that national security was in peril because of the substandard education in American public schools and called for raising standards, increasing rigor, and extending the school day and year. Within two years of the report, more than 300 state and national task forces had investigated the condition of public education in America. Five years later, President Reagan convened dignitaries to celebrate the flurry of reform efforts. As a reporter for the *New York Times* recounts, "Leading politicians and educators, as well as those in the national media who cover education, used the occasion to reflect on the accomplishments of the school reform. And we came to a startling conclusion: There *weren't* any" (Fiske, 1992, p. 25).

In 1989 President George H. W. Bush convened the nation's governors for a national summit on education that resulted in the declaration of ambitious goals for America's schools to be achieved by the year 2000. Among those goals was increasing the high school graduation rate to 90 percent and ensuring the nation's students would be first in the world in math and science achievement. The primary strategy for achieving them, according to President Bush (1989), was "decentralization of authority and decision-making responsibility to the school site, so that educators are empowered to determine the means for accomplishing the goals and are to be held accountable for accomplishing them." The end of the century came and went and, unfortunately, there was virtually no evidence to suggest that any progress had been made toward these ambitious goals.

When President George W. Bush took office, he opted for a very different approach to school reform. Since decentralization of authority had failed to produce the desired results, President Bush launched the most ambitious federal educational initiative in American history, No Child Left Behind (NCLB). The law stipulated that schools must show improving student achievement on standardized tests until not a single student failed to demonstrate proficiency, and it outlined a series of increasingly punitive penalties and sanctions for schools that were unable to do so. The details of what students were to learn, what constituted proficiency, and how they were to be assessed were left up to each of the states to resolve.

By the time Bush left office in 2008, even the original advocates of NCLB concluded it had failed to improve student achievement. A former Bush advisor admitted he had gone from being a "true believer" about the power of NCLB to transform schools to "gradually and reluctantly coming to the conclusion that NCLB as enacted is fatally flawed and probably beyond repair" (Petrilli, 2007). Diane Ravitch, another advocate for the initiative, admitted that the evidence was compelling and conclusive: NCLB had not only failed to improve schools but had damaged them. A disappointed Ravitch (2010a) concluded:

The great legacy of No Child Left Behind is that it has left us with a system of institutionalized fraud. And the institutionalized fraud is that No Child Left Behind has mandated that every child is going to be proficient by the year 2014. . . . And the states are told, "If you don't reach that bar, you're going to be punished. Schools will be closed. They'll be turned into charter schools." That's part of the federal mandate, that schools will be privatized if they can't meet that impossible goal. So in order to preserve some semblance of public education, the states have been encouraged to lie, and many of them are lying, and so we see states that are saying, "90 percent of our kids are proficient in reading," and then when the national test comes out, it's 25 percent.

The Obama administration has cited the improvement of schools as a national imperative, has established the goal of ensuring every high school graduate is "college ready and career ready," and has offered some proposals for amending NCLB. It may be premature to assess the effectiveness of the administration's strategies at this point, but those strategies do have a familiar ring—accountability based on test scores, increasing the number of charter schools, and punishment as motivation, particularly for the five thousand lowest-performing schools in the nation that would be closed according to the Obama plan. The administration is offering educators a carrot along with the stick in the form of billions of dollars in "Race to the Top" funds to be distributed to states on the basis of competitive grants; however, performance pay for teachers and evaluating their performance on the basis of student achievement appear to be prerequisites for consideration.

Michael Fullan (2010a) has been one of the most thoughtful critics of the American school reform effort. As he points out, the fact that "the nation has steadily lost ground to other countries" since the reform efforts were launched "tells you the strategies are dramatically wanting" (p. 22). Nor is he optimistic about the potential outcome of the Obama strategy, stating bluntly, "The stimulus money, *in the absence of an appropriate whole system reform conception,* will fail" (p. 29).

Flawed Strategies Flow From Flawed Assumptions

The strategies set forth to improve education in the United States have not been created in a vacuum; they reflect a certain assumption regarding the problems with education and what must be done to address them. Consider the following strategies and their underlying assumption:

- We need to shake educators from the lethargy inherent in their monopoly by creating more charter schools to compete with public schools (despite a recent report that concluded, "this study reveals in unmistakable terms that, in the aggregate, charter school students are not faring as well as students in traditional public schools" [Center for Research on Education Outcomes, 2009, p. 6]).

- We need to put more pressure on public schools by providing parents with vouchers so they can transfer their students to other schools (even though the evidence demonstrates that "when offered a chance to leave their failing schools . . . less than 5 percent—and in some cases, less than 1 percent—of students actually sought to transfer" [Ravitch, 2010b]).

- We need to hold educators more accountable by creating thirty-seven different ways for schools to fail (even though the increasing number of schools designated as failing each year has demonstrated the futility of this strategy).

- We need to provide financial incentives through performance pay programs that reward individual teachers on the basis of student achievement (even though an analysis of the impact of merit pay for teachers concluded the following:

> You don't have to read the evidence from liter-
> ally decades of research to spot the problems
> with merit pay for schoolteachers. That evidence
> shows that merit-pay plans seldom last longer than
> five years and that merit pay consistently fails to
> improve student performance. The very logic of
> merit pay for teachers suggests that it won't do
> what it is intended to do. (Pfeffer & Sutton, 2006,
> p. 23)

The unspoken assumption behind these strategies is that educators have had the ability to help all students learn, but have lacked sufficient motivation to put forth the effort to help them learn. If that assumption is correct, then perhaps steps to provide sanctions and incentives to spur greater effort might be effective.

We do not, however, believe that the problems of public schools have been caused by the unwillingness of educators to work hard or because they are disinterested in the well-being of their students. The problem, instead, is that they have lacked the collective capacity to promote learning for all students in the existing structures and cultures of the systems in which they work.

School Improvement Means People Improvement

More than a quarter century ago, Ernest Boyer, one of the most influential figures in the advancement of public education and teacher training, observed:

> When you talk about school improvement, you are
> talking about people improvement. That is the only
> way to improve schools, unless you mean painting
> the buildings and fixing the floors. But that's not the
> school: it is the shell. The school is people, so when we
> talk about excellence or improvement or progress, we
> are really talking about the people who make up the
> building. (quoted in Sparks, 1984, p. 35)

More recent research has reaffirmed Boyer's position. A study of the world's best-performing school systems concluded, "The quality of an education system cannot exceed the quality of its teachers" (Barber & Mourshed, 2007, p. 4). Two different meta-analyses of research on the factors that impact student achievement found that the quality of instruction students receive in their classrooms is the most important variable in student achievement. Those same studies also note the wide disparity in the quality of that instruction within the same school (Hattie, 2009; Marzano, 2003). As Hattie wrote:

> The message is simple—what teachers *do* matters. However, this has become a cliché that masks the fact that the greatest source of variance in our system relates to teachers—they can vary in many ways. The codicil is that what "some" teachers do matters. . . . The current mantra is that *teachers make the difference*. . . . This message, like most simple solutions, is not quite right. . . . Not all teachers are effective, not all teachers are experts, and not all teachers have powerful effects on students. (p. 34)

Hattie (2009) described effective teaching in this way:

> The act of teaching requires deliberate interventions to ensure that there is cognitive change in the student: thus the key ingredients are awareness of the learning intentions, knowing when a student is successful in attaining those intentions, having sufficient understanding of the student's understanding as he or she comes to the task, and knowing enough about the content to provide meaningful and challenging experiences in some sort of progressive development. It involves an experienced teacher who knows a range of learning strategies to provide the students when they seem not to understand. (p. 23)

In addition to these pedagogical skills, effective teachers have high expectations for student achievement. They believe that the ability of students to learn is changeable rather than fixed, and they are able to foster the effort that leads to achievement. They create a warm socioemotional climate in their classrooms in which all students are engaged and errors are not only tolerated but are welcomed. They are able to express the intended learning outcomes and success criteria in terms students can understand, and the students themselves recognize the high quality of teaching they are receiving (Hattie, 2009).

Most adults can remember a teacher like this, and we remain grateful for our experience with that teacher. But what happens when even the best-intentioned, hardest-working teachers simply lack the ability to provide this kind of classroom and instruction? No legislative action can mandate that they teach better, nor will threats of sanctions and punishment provide them with greater skills. The world's best school systems recognize that "one cannot give what one does not have" (Barber & Mourshed, 2007, p. 16), and so they focus their school improvement initiatives on creating conditions to improve the professional practice of educators.

If the fundamental challenge of school improvement is improving professional practice, then strategies based on sanctions and punishment must be replaced with strategies to develop the capacity of educators to become more effective. Let's consider three of the strategies that have been offered:

1. Stipulate that teachers present scripted lessons for prescribed curricula with fidelity.

   One strategy being used with increasing frequency, particularly in low-performing schools, is the attempt to translate effective instructional practice into scripts that teachers must follow faithfully as they teach prescribed curricula. After all, if some teachers are highly effective, shouldn't less-capable teachers be required to mimic them? The idea that teaching can be reduced to a script, a checklist, or even a specific methodology has been refuted by some of the world's leading authorities on effective instruction

(Hattie, 2009; Marzano, 2009b; Popham, 2009a). We will have more to say on this later, but for the moment, we suggest that this strategy neither improves professional practice nor generates the necessary commitment to do so.

2. Recruit more capable people to the profession.

Some of the top-performing nations in the world on international assessments recruit teachers from the top quarter of their graduating classes, pay them high starting salaries, and afford the profession considerable status. Thus, it has been suggested that the United States can reform its schools if it adopts similar practices. We can enthusiastically endorse this effort, but it will not solve the immediate challenges facing schools for several reasons.

First, if the answer to the problems of schooling lies solely in those who can be attracted to the profession in the future, we will lose another generation of students to high dropout rates and low academic achievement. Second, if the structure and culture of schools remain the same, bringing new individuals into that environment is more likely to change the people than the environment. As Pfeffer and Sutton (2006) concluded in their study of effective organizations, "Wide-ranging research . . . show[s] it is impossible for even the most talented people to do competent, let alone brilliant, work in a flawed system" (p. 96).

The Teach for America program serves as an example. This program recruits "outstanding recent college graduates from all backgrounds and career interests to commit to teach for two years in urban and rural public schools" and provides them with "the training and ongoing support necessary to ensure their success as teachers in low-income communities" (Teach for America, 2010). Unfortunately, this effort to attract these higher achievers to teaching fails to keep them there. The average tenure in their initial placement is less than the two-year commitment, fewer than half return to their schools for a third year, and only about one-third remain in the profession for more than four years (Harvard Graduate School of Education, 2008). Those opting to leave teaching reported that one of the major factors in their decision was their workplace conditions.

The challenge confronting public education is not recruiting more good people to an ineffective system, but rather creating powerful systems that allow ordinary people to achieve success. The effort to bring qualified people into the field must be accompanied by a concerted effort to make the profession more satisfying and fulfilling.

Finally, and very importantly, recruiting outstanding individuals to a career in education will not result in great schools, because improving student achievement across an entire school or district requires a *collective* effort rather than a series of isolated individual efforts. We will have much more to say about this in later chapters.

3. Focus improvement efforts on building the collective capacity of educators to meet the challenges they face.

Fullan (2010a) considers collective capacity "the break-through concept" (p. 71) vital to substantive school reform because "it enables ordinary people to accomplish extraordinary things" (p. 72). This strategy is not based on the premise that educators have been indifferent to the learning of their students or that they must be replaced by a new generation of educators before students can learn at higher levels. Instead it seeks to create the structures and cultures by which current educators continuously improve both their individual and collective professional practice. Improvement strategies based on building collective capacity regard educators as the solution to, rather than the cause of, the complex problems confronting public education.

A commitment to building collective capacity requires school environments in which the professional learning of educators is:

› Ongoing and sustained rather than episodic

› Job-embedded rather than separate from the work and external to the school

› Specifically aligned with school and district goals rather than the random pursuit of trendy topics

› Focused on improved results rather than projects and activities

› Viewed as a collective and collaborative endeavor rather than an individual activity (Annenberg Institute for School Reform, 2005; Elmore, 2003; McLaughlin & Talbert, 2006; National Staff Development Council, 2001; Teaching Commission, 2004; WestEd, 2000)

Perhaps most importantly, the most effective professional development is specifically designed to result in the improvement of "schools and school systems, not just the improvement of the individuals who work in them" (Elmore, 2003, p. 96).

Creating the Conditions for Continuous School Improvement

This brings us to the assumptions that will drive this book:

• Schools can only be as good as the people within them.

• If one of the most important variables in student learning is the quality of instruction students receive each day, then schools must utilize strategies that result in more good teaching in more classrooms more of the time.

• If substantive school improvement requires a coordinated, systematic, and collective effort rather than a series of isolated individual efforts, then schools and districts must use professional development strategies that are specifically designed to develop the *collective* capacity of educators to meet the needs of students. Strategies based on sanctions, punishments, attracting future generations of educators, or rewarding individual teachers will do little to build the collective capacity of current educators to meet the demands being placed on them.

- The best strategy for improving schools and districts is developing the collective capacity of educators to function as members of a professional learning community (PLC)—a concept based on the premise that if students are to learn at higher levels, processes must be in place to ensure the ongoing, job-embedded learning of the adults who serve them.

- Creating the conditions that foster high-performing PLCs can be done within existing resources if schools and districts are willing to change some of their traditional practices.

The potential of the PLC process to improve schools has repeatedly been cited not only by researchers but also by the professional organizations that serve as advocates for teachers and principals. For a comprehensive list of citations from researchers and organizations that have endorsed the PLC process as a key strategy for improving schools, visit www.allthingsplc.info/tools/print.php#15 and click on "Advocates for PLCs."

The growing recognition of the potential of the PLC process to impact student achievement in a powerful and positive way has helped bring the term *professional learning community* into the common vocabulary of educators throughout the world. But while the term has become widespread, the underlying practices have not, and many of the schools that proudly proclaim to be PLCs do none of the things PLCs actually do. It is difficult to implement a substantive process in any organization when people have a deep understanding of the process and its implications for specific action; it is impossible to do so when there is ambiguity or only a superficial understanding of what must be done (Pfeffer & Sutton, 2000).

Some educators approach the PLC process as if it were a program, simply one more addition to the existing practices of the school. It is not a program. Others regard it as a meeting, as in, "We do PLCs on Wednesdays from 9:00 a.m. to 10:00 a.m., and then we return to business as usual." It is not a meeting. Still others equate a PLC to a book club, as in, "We all read the same book and talk about it." It is not a book club.

The PLC concept represents *"an ongoing process* in which educators work collaboratively in recurring cycles of collective inquiry and action research to achieve better results for the students they serve" (DuFour, DuFour, Eaker, & Many, 2010). It is not a program to be purchased; it is a process to be pursued but never quite perfected. It is not an appendage to existing structures and cultures; it profoundly impacts structure and culture. It is not a meeting; it is "an ethos that infuses every single aspect of a school's operation" (Hargreaves, 2004, p. 48). It does not demand that educators work harder at what they traditionally have done; it calls upon all educators—every teacher, counselor, principal, central office staff member, and superintendent—to redefine their roles and responsibilities and do differently.

Three Big Ideas That Drive the PLC Process

The Professional Learning Community at Work™ process that we advocate rests on three big ideas, and each of those ideas has significant implications for educators.

Big Idea One

The first big idea is that the fundamental purpose of our school is to ensure that all students learn at high levels. In order to bring this idea to life, educators work together to clarify:

- What is it we want our students to know? What knowledge, skills, and dispositions must all students acquire as a result of this grade level, this course, and this unit we are about to teach? What systems have we put in place to ensure we are providing every student with access to a guaranteed and viable curriculum regardless of the teacher to whom that student might be assigned?

- How will we know if our students are learning? How can we check for understanding on an ongoing basis in our individual classrooms? How will we gather evidence of each student's proficiency as a team? What criteria will we establish to assess the quality of student work? How can we be certain we can apply the criteria consistently?

- How will we respond when students do not learn? What steps can we put in place to provide students who struggle with additional time and support for learning in a way that is timely, directive, and systematic rather than invitational and random? How can we provide students with multiple opportunities to demonstrate learning?

- How will we enrich and extend the learning for students who are proficient? How can we differentiate instruction among us so that the needs of all students are being met without relying on rigid tracking?

It is imperative to note that the emphasis placed on student learning in a PLC does not diminish the importance of teaching. In fact, the primary reason to become a PLC is to impact and improve teaching. Too many school reforms have swirled around but not within the classroom. The PLC process is specifically intended to create the conditions that help educators become more skillful in teaching because great teaching and high levels of learning go hand in hand.

Big Idea Two

The second big idea is that if we are to help all students learn, it will require us to work collaboratively in a collective effort to meet the needs of each student. In order to bring this idea to life:

- Educators are organized into meaningful collaborative teams in which members work interdependently to achieve common goals for which they are mutually accountable.

- Regular time for collaboration is embedded into the routine practices of the school.

- Educators are clear on the purpose and priorities of their collaboration. They stay focused on the right work.

- School and district leaders demonstrate "reciprocal accountability" (Elmore, 2003, p. 93). They provide teachers and principals with the resources, training, and ongoing support to help them succeed in implementing the PLC process.

Big Idea Three

The third big idea is that educators must create a results orientation in order to know if students are learning and to respond appropriately to their needs. They must be hungry for evidence of student learning and use that evidence to drive continuous improvement of the PLC process. In order to bring this idea to life:

- Every member of the organization works collaboratively with others to achieve SMART goals that are (1) strategically aligned with school and district goals, (2) measurable, (3) attainable, (4) results-oriented (that is, requiring evidence of higher levels of student learning in order to be achieved), and (5) time bound (O'Neill & Conzemius, 2005).

- Every member of the organization works collaboratively with others to gather and analyze evidence of student learning on a regular basis to *inform and improve his or her professional practice as well as the collective practice of the collaborative team.* Members of the team explore questions such as these: Who among us is getting excellent results teaching this skill? How can we learn from one another? In what area are our students having the most difficulty?

What must we learn as a team in order to better address that area of difficulty?

- Evidence of student learning is used on a regular basis to identify the specific needs of individual students. The school moves beyond using data to make general observations about the achievement of all students. It creates processes to use assessment results to respond to students by name and by need.

- Educators throughout the school assess the effectiveness of every policy, program, procedure, and practice on the basis of its impact on student learning.

Conclusion

As educators throughout North America are beset by the perfect storm of challenging conditions, they would be wise to remember the words of Abraham Lincoln who wrote in his 1862 message to Congress: "The dogmas of the quiet past are inadequate to the stormy present. The occasion is piled high with difficulty, and we must rise to the occasion. As our case is new, so must we think anew" (Lincoln, 1953, p. 537).

The subsequent chapters are based on the premise that if educators are to rise to the occasion and meet the challenges confronting them, they will be required both to think anew and *act* anew. Let's begin by examining how effective leaders contribute to successful implementation of the PLC process at the district level.

CHAPTER 2

The District's Role in Supporting the PLC Process

It should come as no surprise that one result of the multiplicity of activities (in districts that demonstrated dramatic gains in student achievement) was a collaborative, professional school culture. . . . Leaders understood that the way to attain their ambitious goals was developing a collaborative and professional school culture, what is commonly called a "professional learning community" today.

—**Allan R. Odden and Sarah J. Archibald**

In the late 1970s and early 1980s, researchers Ron Edmonds, Wilbur Brookover, Michael Rutter, and Larry Lezotte began to challenge the conclusions of earlier studies that asserted educators had little or no influence on student learning. They presented evidence that some schools were, in fact, significantly more effective than others in helping students from similar backgrounds learn at high levels, and they identified first five and then seven conditions that correlated with more effective schools. This Effective Schools Research focused on the climate, culture, and practices of the individual school and ignored the school district.

Lezotte (2008) admits that initially, he and his colleagues alleged the district office was "irrelevant" when it came to developing effective schools. As he explained:

When we found an effective school, it was likely in a district with many other schools, none of which were effective yet all had the same board, superintendent

and central office. Furthermore, we proclaimed that a
school staff could implement the correlates of effective schools at any time. No particular outside help or
support was required, since no outside help or support
was found to be associated with the schools that were
already found to be effective. (pp. 13–14)

In time, however, the researchers found schools could not remain
effective without the support of the central office. A principal and
key staff could help a school improve student achievement through
heroic effort, but they could not sustain the improvement or survive the departure of key leaders without the support of the district and a commitment at that level to promote effective schooling
practices (Lezotte, 2008).

More recently, district leadership has been found to have "a
measurable effect on student achievement" (Marzano & Waters,
2009, p. 12) and to be vital to improving school systems (Louis,
Leithwood, Wahlstrom, & Anderson, 2010; Mourshed, Chijioke, &
Barber, 2010). Furthermore, the strategies central office leaders utilize to support improved student achievement in schools throughout a school system have become much more explicit.

Effective District Leaders Both Direct and Empower

The site-based school improvement model was based on the
premise that if educators were given unfettered autonomy in their
schools, innovation and creativity would flourish. Educators would
approach their challenges with a renewed sense of enthusiasm,
ownership, and commitment if they were given the freedom to
identify the problems in their own schools and were empowered
to develop their own solutions.

This premise proved faulty. Educators in schools with site-based
autonomy were no more likely to engage in matters essential to
teaching and learning than their more rigidly supervised counterparts (Kruse, Seashore Louis, & Bryk, 1995). Even if an individual

school was able to demonstrate improvement, its practices never influenced the rest of the system because there was no process for sharing knowledge across schools. Furthermore, the commitment to each school's autonomy meant individual schools were free to ignore evidence of more effective practices in other schools (Elmore, 2003). And as we mentioned previously, schools that did experience short-term gains were unable to sustain them.

A meta-analysis of research on site-based management actually found a negative correlation with student achievement, indicating that "an increase in site-based management is associated with a *decrease* in student achievement" (Marzano & Waters, 2009, p. 4). As one review concluded, "Much harm has been done to public education and to the ideas of equity and excellence" by poor implementation of site-based management (Schlechty, 2005).

Improvement effort driven by top-down directives from the central office proved no more effective in raising student achievement. This approach failed to "garner ownership, commitment or even clarity about the nature of the reforms" (Fullan, 2007, p. 11). Furthermore, principals and teachers proved adept at ignoring the mandates, closing the doors to their schools and classrooms, and continuing with business as usual (Tyack & Cuban, 1995).

Effective school district leaders have resolved this bottom-up versus top-down dilemma by embracing the concept of "defined autonomy" (Marzano & Waters, 2009) or "simultaneous loose-tight leadership" (DuFour, DuFour, Eaker, & Many, 2010). In these districts, superintendents work with the board of education, other central office administrators, and principals to articulate clear, *nondiscretionary* student achievement goals for the district as a whole, for each school, and for subgroups of students. These districts also establish a common framework of research-based strategies for achieving those goals.

The willingness to articulate fundamental goals, the strategies for achieving those goals, and the indicators that will be used to monitor progress toward the goals are vital to effective district leadership. A study of high-performing school systems around the world concluded that, in every instance, the first step effective leaders took to improve their systems was to clarify "what was non-negotiable." Although these leaders were willing to compromise in many specific aspects of systemwide improvement, they were vigilant in ensuring "there was little or no compromise in the execution" of the non-negotiables (Mourshed et al., 2010, p. 110).

In effective districts, educators in individual schools enjoy some latitude within specified parameters, and the unique context of an individual school is recognized. But the district leadership establishes the "common work of schools within the district" that serves as the "glue holding the district together" (Marzano & Waters, 2009, p. 90). The superintendent expects building principals to accept responsibility for the success of their schools and provides principals with some flexibility, but principals are also expected to "lead *within the boundaries established by the district's goals*" (Marzano & Waters, 2009, p. 8).

Fairfax County Public Schools, the largest school district in Virginia with more than 275 school sites, serves as an example. The board of education adopted a policy stipulating that the primary strategy for achieving the district's ambitious goals was to operate each of its schools as a PLC. Over time, it became evident, however, that simply adopting a policy endorsing the PLC process did not provide the specificity and clarity needed to impact practice at the school site. So the central office leadership team worked with a representative group of principals to identify specific PLC practices they expected to see in each school, because those practices could be directly tied to increases in student learning. Their dialogue resulted in a document titled the "Fairfax County Shared Vision of Professional Learning Communities—Fundamental Elements," which is presented in part in figure 2.1 on pages 31–32.

Part 1: Learning as Our Fundamental Purpose
We acknowledge that the fundamental purpose of our school is to help all students achieve high levels of learning, and therefore, we are willing to examine all of our practices in light of their impact on learning. The priorities for our shared work will include the following: • Schools will build collective knowledge regarding state standards and the FCPS Program of Studies to clarify what all students must know and be able to do as a result of each unit of instruction. • Schools will develop and deploy frequent team-developed common assessments to monitor the learning of each student on all essential outcomes. These assessments will be aligned to the required state and district tests. • Schools will dedicate and structure time to implement intervention/enrichment initiatives during the course of the regular school day and academic year. • Schools will provide a system of mandatory interventions based on the examined evidence that guarantees each student receives additional time and support for learning until he or she has met the agreed-upon standards. Intervention efforts will be monitored and adjusted, as needed, using a regular cycle of data analysis.
Part 2: Building a Collaborative Culture Through High-Performing Teams
We are committed to working together to achieve our collective purpose of learning for all students. We will cultivate a collaborative culture through the development of high-performing teams. The priorities for our shared work will include the following: • Schools will ensure that collaborative teams are given time during the contractual day and year to meet on a regular basis. • Schools will work in collaborative teams interdependently to clarify what students must learn, gather evidence of student learning, analyze the evidence, identify the most powerful teaching strategies/best practices, and transfer these strategies across all team members.

Figure 2.1: Fairfax County Shared Vision of Professional Learning Communities—Fundamental Elements.

Continued on next page →

- Schools will ensure that collaborative teams develop and implement, where appropriate, unified policies and procedures regarding content scope, sequencing, pacing, grading, and other assessment practices.

- School collaborative teams will work together interdependently to create and achieve common SMART goals as part of the strategic planning process.

Part 3: A Focus on Results

We assess our effectiveness on the basis of results rather than intentions. Individuals, teams, and schools seek relevant data and information and use that information to promote continuous improvement. The priorities for our shared work will include the following:

- Schools will analyze data from common assessments to identify students who need additional time and support for learning, discover strengths and weaknesses in their individual and collective teaching, and help measure team progress toward its common goals.

- Schools will act on the information from their data using a research-based methodology such as the Plan, Do, Study, Act (PDSA) model to increase teacher/team effectiveness and ensure that all students learn and benefit from our collective best efforts as we close all achievement gaps.

The Fairfax document acknowledges that although schools need to ensure these essential elements are in place, there is room for latitude at the school site because there are multiple pathways for proceeding. For example, while the district calls for the development of high-performing collaborative teams in every school, there are a variety of ways schools could organize teachers into teams—by course, by grade level, by department, interdisciplinary, vertically, partnered with other schools, or electronically. Schools have the autonomy to decide how they will organize staff members into teams, but they do not have the discretion to allow teachers to work in isolation.

The Need for Specificity

Even in districts that hope to implement the PLC process, district leaders often lack a clear understanding of how to engage educators in the work at the school site (Annenberg Institute for School Reform, 2005). Districts tend to rely on generalities ("We want all schools to focus on teaching and learning") rather than clarifying the actionable steps they expect schools to take and the evidence they must present to demonstrate that the steps have been taken. A gap exists between the strategic vision and the specifics of bringing the vision to life (Louis et al., 2010).

The Fairfax leaders have addressed that lack of clarity by going beyond esoteric statements of philosophy or a listing of unassailable beliefs. District leaders have delineated some very specific practices and processes that are to be established in every school. Furthermore, the district has articulated specific learning goals for all students and has established a process to ensure that each school adopts student achievement targets that align with district goals. Again, schools have a considerable degree of autonomy in determining how they will meet the district's expectations, but the district was not reluctant to be directive when stating those expectations.

Fullan (2010c) has assured leaders that "it's okay to be assertive" (p. 30). We believe that it is not only okay; it is imperative. Effective district leaders will build shared knowledge throughout the organization as to why an improvement initiative is needed and will create guiding coalitions to help champion the initiative. At some point, however, they will be direct and explicit about the goals that are to be achieved and a few critical conditions they expect to see in every school, because a culture of *defined* autonomy ultimately calls upon leaders to *define* what is to be tight throughout the district.

When working with specific districts, Rick often asks first the central office staff, and then principals, to list three things that people throughout the organization understand are "tight"—nondiscretionary priorities that must be observed in every school.

Superintendents are typically stunned to discover that not a single answer appears on the majority of the lists. A district cannot experience the benefits of defined autonomy when confusion reigns regarding nondiscretionary priorities. Central office leaders must not only clarify those priorities but should be vigilant in monitoring the degree to which the priorities are understood and acted on throughout the district.

Effective District Leaders Create a Common Language

Creating a common, widely understood language is an important element in any substantive change process (Kegan & Lahey, 2001; Pfeffer & Sutton, 2000). Effective districts are attentive to developing a shared understanding of a common vocabulary about practice (Marzano & Waters, 2009; McLaughlin & Talbert, 2006). Although this sounds relatively simple, many districts settle for the use of jargon without developing a common understanding of *the implications for specific action* behind the terms. *Differentiated instruction, response to intervention, formative assessment,* and *professional learning communities* are just a few examples of terms commonly being used in districts where educators have no clear or consistent understanding of what those terms mean.

Leaders who develop a common language do not settle for a superficial use of key terms. Instead, they drill deeper to ensure there is understanding behind each term. To illustrate, consider the following imaginary exchange between a principal and superintendent:

> Principal: "You said you want all of our schools to focus on student learning. But what does that really mean? What does a focus on learning look like?"
>
> Superintendent: "There are certain indicators that would show a school has a focus on learning. For example, teachers in the school are working together in collaborative teams to ensure they are providing students with a guaranteed and viable curriculum.

The school could provide evidence that each student's learning is being monitored on a continuous basis through the use of ongoing formative assessments in the classroom and frequent common formative assessments developed by the team. Each team could demonstrate that its members have clarified the criteria they use in judging the quality of student work and have established inter-rater reliability in assessing student work. The school would have an intervention plan to provide students who struggle with additional time and support for learning in a way that is timely, directive, precise, and systematic. It would have a coordinated strategy to enrich and extend the learning for students who were proficient. Members of the collaborative team would use evidence of student learning to inform and improve their individual and collective professional practice and to make progress toward their SMART goals. These are the kinds of things we would see in a school that demonstrated a focus on learning."

This response is insightful and relatively concise, but it will be of little help to the principal unless he or she and the superintendent have a shared understanding of such terms as *collaborative team, guaranteed and viable curriculum, formative assessment, common assessment, inter-rater reliability, intervention, directive, systematic, enrichment, proficient, collective professional practice,* and *SMART goal.* In that single paragraph, there are at least a dozen terms and phrases that can obscure rather than promote clarity. Furthermore, educators are far more prone to feign understanding and talk through and around the issues rather than acknowledge the concepts are unclear.

The relationship between a student's understanding of key vocabulary terms and his or her academic achievement has been well established in research (Marzano, 2004). Actually teaching learners the meaning of important terms they will encounter in their upcoming work can dramatically impact their success because "direct instruction in vocabulary works" (Marzano, 2004, p. 68).

Among the most effective strategies for teaching essential vocabulary are identifying a list of terms critical to the learners' academic success; providing a description, explanation, and example of the term; and engaging learners in discussion of the term.

The same principle applies to those who are attempting to lead the PLC process. If district leaders are to succeed in building a common language, they should identify the key terms people throughout the organization must understand in order to move forward; directly teach those terms through description, explanation, and examples; engage staff in discussions of the terms; and periodically assess levels of understanding.

Figure 2.2 provides examples of key terms for PLCs. If people throughout the organization have a shared understanding of those terms, they will significantly increase the likelihood of their success in implementing the PLC process. Visit www.allthingsplc.info for a glossary of these and other terms.

Professional learning community
Defined autonomy
Collaborative team
Guaranteed and viable curriculum
Essential learnings
Balanced assessment
Common assessment
Formative assessment
Performance-based assessment
Inter-rater reliability
Systematic intervention
SMART goal
Simultaneous loose and tight culture
Four critical questions that drive the work of teams
Three big ideas of a PLC
Collective inquiry
Action research

Figure 2.2: Key terms in implementing the PLC process.

Effective District Leaders Monitor the PLC Process in Each School as They Develop the Capacity of Principals to Lead the Process

Creating a PLC will always require a collective effort, but the fate of that effort will depend to a large extent on the leadership capabilities of the principal. A highly effective principal can have a "dramatic impact on overall student achievement in a school" (Marzano, Waters, & McNulty, 2005, p. 10), and principals play the key role in creating the conditions that determine whether the PLC process will flourish or perish (McLaughlin & Talbert, 2006). As Robert Evans (2001) wrote:

> Principals are widely seen as indispensable to innovation. No reform effort, however worthy, survives a principal's indifference or opposition. When they are asked to lead projects they don't fully grasp or endorse, they are likely to be ambivalent. Central office must remember the importance of allowing time for principals to thrash out their questions as they relate to changes. (p. 202)

If superintendents are to succeed in implementing the PLC process in schools throughout the district, they must establish a framework for building the individual and collective capacity of principals to lead the process successfully (Louis et al., 2010). The ability of principals to transform their schools into PLCs and their willingness to focus their effort and energy on that challenge is likely to vary widely in schools within the same district. Effective superintendents "decrease the variability of the leadership across schools in the district" (Marzano & Waters, 2009, p. 89) not only by clarifying expectations for principals but also by providing them with the ongoing training and support to meet those expectations.

Some of the most powerful strategies for giving principals the tools and support they need to succeed in leading a PLC are as follows:

- Superintendents help principals come to a deeper understanding of the PLC process by providing them with initial training, sending them to visit schools that are functioning as high-performing PLCs, leading them in reading books and articles on the process, and engaging them in two-way dialogue about their questions and concerns. The first step in developing the ability of principals to lead the PLC process is to make them aware of the process and what it requires of them to implement it.

- As we mentioned previously, superintendents clarify the specific conditions they expect principals to create in their schools and build a common vocabulary regarding essential terms in the PLC process.

- Superintendents turn the district principals' meetings into a collaborative and collective effort to identify and resolve implementation challenges. They use these meetings to rehearse and role play what principals are called upon to do back in their buildings. For example, prior to asking teams to establish a SMART goal, a principals' meeting would be devoted to helping principals articulate a rationale for SMART goals; gather the tools, templates, and resources they could use to help their teams complete this task; and rehearse a crucial conversation with a team that balks at establishing SMART goals.

- Superintendents monitor the implementation process and help principals identify and address challenges in their schools by requiring principals to explain, in a public forum, the steps they have taken to move the PLC process forward. Each principal is called upon to present evidence to his or her colleagues and the central office regarding how his or her school has addressed the specific conditions that are expected to be evident in all schools. For example, each principal explains how teachers in the school have been organized into teams, how they are given time to collaborate, how the principal monitors the work of the teams, how the results of common formative assessments are being used by teams, and how the school is providing for systematic intervention and enrichment. Principals are also asked to provide artifacts that demonstrate the effectiveness of their teams in such tasks as creating norms, establishing a guaranteed curriculum, and developing common assessments.

- Superintendents create a process to have principals present their colleagues and the central office staff with a comprehensive analysis of evidence of student achievement over a three-year period. Principals are then expected to work collaboratively with their colleagues to learn from each other's successes and help resolve one another's difficulties. This process, when done well, provides the combination of pressure and support that build capacity. The process helps foster collaboration, collective responsibility, a results orientation, and a culture of accountability by capitalizing on the subtle peer pressure that accompanies presenting to one's peers and by making evidence of student learning transparent. And, very importantly, it represents a powerful tool for increasing a principal's effectiveness in leading a PLC because it develops a stronger sense of self-efficacy among principals (Louis et al., 2010).

The key to the effectiveness of the process is using it to inform principals and improve their professional practice rather than ranking or rating them. Whether there are five elementary schools in a district or fifty, if they are compared on the basis of state tests results, one will be ranked first and one will be ranked last. That is inevitable. What is not inevitable is that districts and schools use the information as part of a continuous process to improve achievement. Used in that context, the lowest-performing school in a district could be celebrated for having the greatest gains in student achievement in a given year while the highest-performing school in a district could raise concerns because student achievement has declined for three consecutive years.

The principle of reciprocal accountability that we referenced in chapter 1 applies here. Superintendents must hold principals accountable for leading the PLC process, but they must also be accountable *to* principals for providing them with the training and support to succeed. The initial assumption that should guide superintendents is that principals would prefer to be effective and those who are not simply require additional training and more focused support to be effective. District leaders should view the challenge of implementation as one of capacity building, and they should invest in this ongoing, job-embedded, collaborative learning among their principals rather than relying solely on external training (Louis et al., 2010).

If, however, it becomes evident over time that a principal is unwilling or unable to lead, effective districts will remove that individual from the position. In these districts it is understood that principals must be able to lead a process of continuous improvement (Fullan, 2010b). The principalship is simply too important to the quality of a school to tolerate weak and ineffective leadership.

Effective Superintendents Limit Initiatives

One of the biggest impediments to improving schools is the unmanageable number of initiatives pursued by the central office and the total lack of coherence among those initiatives (Olson, 2007). In too many districts, the adage "What gets monitored gets done" has been misinterpreted as, "The more programs we monitor, the more that will get done." As a result, educators throughout North America are suffering from what Doug Reeves (2011) has called "initiative fatigue" as they grapple with the multitude of fragmented, disconnected, short-term projects that sap their energy.

Effective districts identify a few key priorities and then pursue them relentlessly (Fullan, 2010b). They make the PLC process *the* strategy for school improvement rather than one of fifteen different initiatives. There are certainly multiple elements to the PLC process—organizing staff into relevant collaborative teams, establishing a guaranteed curriculum, creating common formative assessments, analyzing evidence of student learning to improve adult practice, creating systems of intervention and enrichment—but these elements are part of one coherent strategy to improve schools. Effective superintendents stress coherence rather than presenting these critical elements as disconnected tasks, and they buffer the school from other improvement initiatives.

Developing districtwide capacity to operate schools as PLCs demands not only an effort that is coordinated and focused but also one that is sustained over an extended period of time (Fullan, 2010b). The districts that improve student achievement recognize the "critical importance of patience and sustained, continual efforts aimed at improvement" (Louis et al., 2010, p. 213). Superintendents are well advised to "spend ten times more energy reinforcing the change they just made than looking for the next great change to try" (Blanchard, 2007, p. 246).

Doug Reeves (2011) has presented compelling evidence on the link between a sustained focus on limited goals and improved student achievement. After conducting research on more than two thousand schools serving 1.5 million students in the United States and Canada, he concluded:

- "Focus is a prerequisite for school improvement." (p. 14)

- When the relative importance of fifteen different leadership practices was evaluated using factor analysis, focus had the highest relationship to student achievement.

- When focus was combined with effective monitoring and a sense of efficacy on the part of adults in the organization, it yielded "strikingly positive results" (p. 49) for all students and schools regardless of their demographics.

- "Without focus, even the best leadership ideas will fail, the most ideal research-based initiatives will fail, and the most self-sacrificing earnest leaders will fail. Worst of all, without focus by educational leaders, students and teachers will fail." (p. 14)

District leaders must demonstrate the discipline to concentrate
the entire organization's energies on the challenging task of creating a PLC in every school, coordinate all central office services
to support that task, declare a moratorium on new initiatives for
several years, allow staff in each school some leeway in moving
forward with the initiative, and very importantly, maintain their
commitment to this focus over a period of years. The transformation from traditional schools to PLCs does not require the pursuit
of multiple initiatives simultaneously, but it does demand fierce
resolve, tremendous passion, and relentless persistence.

Effective Superintendents Communicate Priorities Effectively

Marcus Buckingham (2005) has concluded that the one thing all
leaders must remember to be effective is the importance of clarity
in their communication. Even if superintendents establish limited
goals and priorities, they will be unable to implement the PLC
process in schools throughout an entire district unless they are
able to communicate those goals and priorities effectively to all
stakeholders.

Effective superintendents recognize the importance of ongoing
communication. A "state of the district" address at the start of the
school year does not suffice. A single presentation on the district's
new direction fails to meet the standard of powerful communication no matter how eloquently it is presented, because ongoing
communication "during implementation is far more important
than communication prior to implementation" (Fullan, 2010a, p.
50). Effective superintendents keep the message simple and consistent. They demonstrate congruency between their own actions
and professed priorities. They ensure the local board of education
is aligned with and supportive of the district's goals and priorities,
and they demand that leaders throughout the district speak with
one voice regarding what is tight because solidarity of leadership

is a key element in successful implementation of an improvement process (Louis et al., 2010; Marzano & Waters, 2009).

For communication to be effective, however, it must go two ways. One of the most consistent lessons that emerges from the research on the change process is the importance of keeping communication channels open because "communication pathways are the veins and arteries of new ideas" (Kouzes & Posner, 1987, p. 56). Effective district leaders engage with stakeholders (Mourshed et al., 2010). They are eager to initiate dialogue, and they develop formal and informal strategies for soliciting the perspectives of others. They are hungry for feedback so they can make adjustments and course corrections. For example, the questions in the following feature box, adapted from DuFour, DuFour, and Eaker (2008), could easily be converted into a survey to help a central office staff gather honest feedback from principals and teachers.

A Communications Audit for the Central Office

What systems have been put in place in our district to ensure priorities are addressed in each school?

- Do we have systems for clarifying what students must learn?

- Do we have systems for monitoring student learning?

- Do we have systems for responding when students have difficulty?

- Do we have systems for enriching and extending learning for students who are proficient?

- Do we have systems for monitoring and supporting teams?

- Do we have systems for providing each teacher and team with the timely information essential to continuous improvement?

- Do we have systems to build the capacity of principals to lead the PLC process?

What do we monitor in our district?

- How do we monitor student learning?
- How do we monitor the work and the effectiveness of our collaborative teams?
- How do we monitor the work and effectiveness of our building administrators?
- How do we monitor the progress each school is making on the PLC journey?
- How do we monitor the work and the effectiveness of the central office?
- How do we monitor the work and effectiveness of the board of education?

What questions do we ask in our district?

- What questions are we asking people to resolve through collective inquiry?
- What questions drive the work of individuals and teams throughout our organizations?
- What questions drive the work of our administrative meetings?
- What questions drive the work of the board of education?

How do we allocate resources (time, money, people) in our district?

- How do we provide time for intervention and enrichment for our students?
- How do we provide time for our collaborative teams to engage in collective inquiry?
- Are we using our financial and human resources most effectively?
- What are high-time/low-leverage activities that we should discontinue because they are not contributing to our goals?

What do we celebrate in our district?

- What process is in place to help identify schools and teams that are improving?

- How do we acknowledge and celebrate improvement?
- Who are the heroes in our district?

What are we willing to confront in our district?

- Have we recognized that confronting behavior that is inconsistent with our district goals and priorities is essential to our credibility?
- Have we recognized that confronting resistance is essential to the clarity of our communication?
- Have we been willing to address the problem of principals or staff members who continue to resist this initiative?

What do we model in our district?

- What evidence shows that the members of the central office are committed to and focused on high levels of learning for all students?
- What evidence shows that that we work together collaboratively?
- How do members of the central office gather and use evidence of results to inform and improve our own practice?
- Have we aligned district practices with district priorities and been willing to change those practices that do not reflect our priorities?

Conclusion

Leadership from the central office matters—both in terms of raising student achievement and in terms of creating the conditions for adult learning that lead to higher levels of student achievement. Without effective leadership from the central office, the PLC process will not become deeply embedded in schools throughout a district. Fortunately, the nature of effective leadership at that level of the organization has come much more sharply into focus, and is characterized by both pressure and support. As Louis and colleagues concluded:

In sum, the analysis suggests that investment in the professional development of school leaders will have limited effects on efficacy and student achievement unless districts also develop clear goals for improvement. On the other hand, setting targets and emphasizing responsibility for achieving them is not likely to produce a payoff for students unless those initiatives are accompanied by leadership development practices that principals perceive as helping them to improve their personal competencies. (2010, p. 145)

Essential to effective district leadership is a strong partnership with capable principals. We turn to the role of the principal in a PLC in the next chapter.

CHAPTER 3

The Principal's Role in Leading a Professional Learning Community

> Principals arguably are the most important players
> affecting the character and consequence of teachers'
> school-site professional communities. Principals are
> culture-makers, intentionally or not.
>
> —Milbrey McLaughlin and Joan Talbert

In chapter 1, we articulated the need for school reform and presented a rationale for the power of the professional learning community (PLC) process to generate and sustain a type and level of reform hitherto not available to K–12 educators. At a very basic level, school reform is about substantively changing people, and PLCs are a necessary condition to this end. Chapter 2 clarified how central office leaders can contribute to this effort in schools throughout a district. This chapter addresses the principal's role in developing the capacity for change using the vehicle of the PLC process. We begin with a brief discussion of the research on school leadership.

The Research on School Leadership

The research supporting the importance of effective school leadership in creating the conditions for effective schooling is growing rapidly. It was not that long ago, however, that some educational researchers and theorists believed principal leadership had little or nothing to do with student achievement. For example, in their meta-analysis of thirty-seven studies from 1986 to 1996 conducted across a variety of countries, Witziers, Bosker, and Kruger (2003) could find no correlation between principal leadership and student achievement and concluded that there is little if any relationship between the quality of the principal's leadership and student learning. They punctuated their point by titling their report "Educational Leadership and Student Achievement: The Elusive Search for an Association."

Since that study, however, other researchers have arrived at very different conclusions. Some of those subsequent studies have even demonstrated why the Witziers and colleagues finding might not apply to the United States. For example, Marzano et al. (2005) noted that the Witziers study averaged correlations from studies across a variety of countries to estimate the overall relationship between leadership and student achievement. Many of those countries have administrative structures quite different from the traditional structure of K–12 schools in the United States. When only those studies that focused on U.S. schools are considered from the Witziers synthesis, the correlation between principal leadership and student achievement is quite positive.

In their meta-analysis of sixty-nine studies conducted from 1978 to 2001, Marzano et al. (2005) found that the average correlation in studies conducted in the United States indicates that principal leadership has a significant and positive relationship with student achievement. Since then other studies have arrived at this same conclusion (see Robinson, 2007).

In short, a justifiable conclusion one can glean from the research is that the more skilled the building principal, the more learning can be expected among students. Stated differently, the research now supports what practitioners have known for decades: powerful school leadership on the part of the principal has a positive effect on student achievement.

Although it is now well accepted in K–12 education in the United States that principal leadership has a significant relationship with student achievement, it is also recognized that the relationship is indirect rather than direct (Marzano & Waters, 2009; Marzano et al., 2005). The actions and behaviors of the principal do not directly affect student learning because principals do not usually provide instruction to students. It is the actions and behaviors of teachers that directly affect student achievement since teachers are the providers of instruction. Consequently, the relationship between principal behavior and student achievement can be depicted as indicated in figure 3.1.

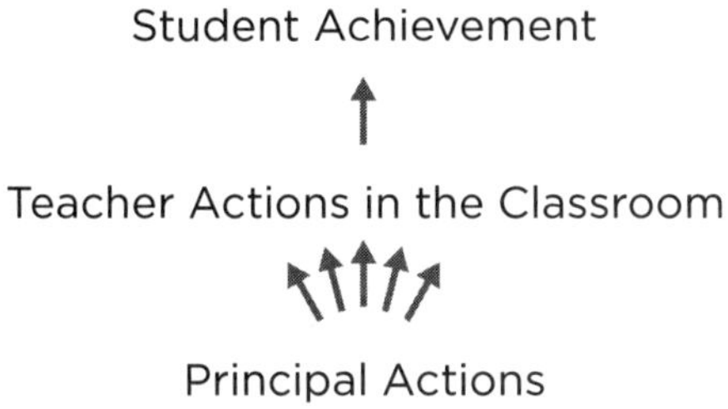

Student Achievement

↑

Teacher Actions in the Classroom

↖↑↑↗↗

Principal Actions

Figure 3.1: Relationship between principal behavior and student achievement.

Figure 3.1 indicates that the principal's influence on student achievement passes through teachers. In other words, the principal affects teachers who in turn have a direct influence on student achievement. One of the more curious aspects of figure 3.1 is that multiple lines of influence are depicted between the principal and teachers' actions. This is because traditionally there has been no way for principals to interact directly and concretely with teachers in a manner that influences their actions in the classroom. Marzano, Water, and McNulty (2005) identified *twenty-one* different responsibilities of the principal that are supported by the research—twenty-one actions that are presumed to have a positive influence on what teachers do. A list of twenty-one multifaceted and disparate responsibilities underscores two of the fundamental historical constraints that well-intentioned principals have confronted in their efforts to be effective school leaders. First, there has been no vehicle that allows them to influence directly what isolated teachers do in the classroom. Second, no one person has the knowledge, skills, or energy to fulfill twenty-one responsibilities simultaneously. Let's examine both of these barriers to effective principal leadership.

A Tradition of Teacher Isolation

The traditional structure of schools and the school day has made it almost impossible for principals to directly influence teachers because those structures have fostered isolated teachers in stand-alone classrooms. Even a cursory review of the research on K–12 education provides evidence of a culture of professional isolation. In his comprehensive study of schooling in the United States, John Goodlad (1984) found that teachers worked in isolation and demonstrated little interest in making what or how they taught subject to analysis, discussion, or improvement. Lieberman and Rosenholtz (1987) agree that "isolation and insulation are the expected conditions in too many schools. These conditions do not foster individual teacher growth and school improvement" (p. 94). A study conducted by the National Commission on Teaching and America's Future (Fulton, Yoon, & Lee, 2005) describes isolated teaching in stand-alone classrooms as the most persistent norm standing in the way of improving schools. Roland Barth (1990) notes that even teachers on the same schedule who use the same materials rarely interact with each other except during a thirty-five-minute lunch period during which informal norms often forbid any kind of professional talk. Elmore (2003) was merely repeating more than thirty years of consistent findings when he wrote:

> The design of work in schools is fundamentally incompatible with the practice of improvement. Teachers spend most of their time working in isolation from each other in self-contained classrooms. . . . The problem with this design is that it provides almost no opportunity for teachers to engage in continuous and sustained learning about their practice in the setting in which they actually work. . . . This disconnect between

the requirements of learning to teach well and the structure of teachers' work life is fatal to any sustained process of instructional improvement. (p. 127)

The tradition of teacher isolation from both colleagues and the principal continues to permeate many schools today. A study commissioned by the Wallace Foundation concluded:

Our evidence also points to the continuing preference of many of teachers to be "left alone." These teachers typically view the presence of a principal in their classrooms as unnecessary and sometimes bothersome. . . . Maintenance of the status quo, which for most secondary school teachers meant not having direct and frequent contact with the principal (or anyone else, for that matter) about ways to improve instruction, was preferred. (Louis et al., 2010, p. 91)

This traditional structure and culture have made it difficult for principals to have an impact on the professional practice of teachers. If a school with fifty classroom teachers has been structured so that those teachers work in isolation, principals will struggle to fulfill their myriad responsibilities to each educator in his or her isolated classroom. Inevitably principals find it almost impossible to serve fifty different masters. Therefore, principals have either struggled to contrive ways to interact with teachers in the hopes of influencing their behavior or have resigned themselves to managing rather than leading their schools.

The PLC process, and the collaborative team structure in particular, are specifically designed to alter this dynamic by changing the traditional practices of schooling. The principal of a K–5 building can now work closely with six teams rather than thirty individuals. The principal of a large high school can influence twenty team leaders directly rather than 150 teachers indirectly. In short, the PLC process provides a vehicle for focused interactions between principals and teachers.

Within the context of the collaborative team structure of a PLC, one might depict the relationship between principal behavior and student achievement as shown in figure 3.2.

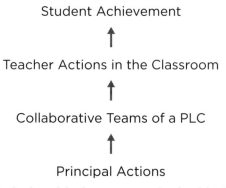

Figure 3.2: Relationship between principal behavior and student achievement with the collaborative teams of a professional learning community.

As depicted in figure 3.2, principals have a direct line of influence to collaborative teams, and teams have a direct line of influence to what occurs in classrooms. A basic tenet of this book is that the PLC process provides a vehicle that allows principals to execute a number of the responsibilities of school leadership in an integrated and focused fashion. In fact, the collaborative teams vital to the PLC process provide a focused venue in which to address nineteen of the original twenty-one responsibilities identified by Marzano, Waters, and McNulty (2005):

1. Providing affirmation and celebration of staff effort and achievement

2. Challenging the status quo as a change agent

3. Establishing processes to ensure effective communication throughout the school

4. Shaping the assumptions, beliefs, expectations, and habits that constitute the school's culture

5. Demonstrating flexibility in meeting the different needs of teams and being willing to make modifications to school procedures

6. Focusing on clear goals and relentlessly pursuing the school's purpose and priorities

7. Articulating the ideals and beliefs that drive the day-to-day work of the school

8. Soliciting input from staff in the design and implementation of procedures and policies

9. Engaging staff in the ongoing review and discussion of the most promising practices for improving student learning

10. Participating in the design and implementation of curriculum, instruction, and assessment

11. Demonstrating interest in and knowledge of curriculum, instruction, and assessment

12. Creating processes to provide ongoing monitoring of the school's practices and their effect on student learning

13. Creating the conditions that optimize school improvement efforts

14. Establishing clear procedures and orderly routines

15. Serving as a spokesperson and advocate for the school and staff

16. Establishing a positive working relationship with each member of the staff

17. Providing teachers with the resources, materials, and support to help them succeed at what they are being asked to do

18. Recognizing the undercurrents of the informal organization of the school and using that information to be proactive in addressing problems and concerns

19. Being visible throughout the school and having positive interactions with staff and students

Only two of the twenty-one responsibilities offered by Marzano, Waters, and McNulty do not naturally have a home in collaborative teams. Those two—contingent rewards and discipline—focus on the principal's interaction with specific individuals. The other nineteen responsibilities, however, most certainly are made easier by and naturally fit within the context of the collaborative team process. We illustrate this connection between the principal's responsibilities and the collaborative team structure in figure 3.3.

Principal Responsibility	Application to Collaborative Teams of PLC
1. Providing affirmation and celebration of staff effort and achievement	Using the goals of each collaborative team to recognize and celebrate progress toward those goals or to identify and overcome obstacles that have prevented the attainment of those goals
2. Challenging the status quo as a change agent	Assisting each team in implementing a continuous improvement process
3. Establishing processes to ensure effective communication throughout the school	Ensuring that each collaborative team has a clear understanding of priorities and access to the principal during PLC meetings and other times
4. Shaping the assumptions, beliefs, expectations, and habits that constitute the school's culture	Creating the conditions that promote collaboration and collective efforts based on shared vision and commitments
5. Demonstrating flexibility in meeting the different needs of teams and being willing to make modifications to school procedures	Recognizing the most appropriate and effective type of guidance and support that is required for individual teams and executing that necessary behavior
6. Focusing on clear goals and relentlessly pursuing the school's purpose and priorities	Ensuring that each collaborative team has identified and is working toward clear SMART goals that can only be achieved if members work interdependently to achieve them

7. Articulating the ideals and beliefs that drive the day-to-day work of the school	Infusing the three strongly held big ideas into the collaborative team process
8. Soliciting input from staff in the design and implementation of procedures and policies	Empowering teams to make important decisions that directly impact the quality of student learning and regularly seeking input from teams regarding schoolwide decisions
9. Engaging staff in the ongoing review and discussion of the most promising practices for improving student learning	Sharing relevant research with teams and engaging them in collective inquiry regarding the instructional strategies that directly impact student learning though action research
10. Participating in the design and implementation of curriculum, instruction, and assessment	Clarifying the work of teams, monitoring that work, and engaging in dialogue with teams on the four critical questions of learning
11. Demonstrating interest in and knowledge of curriculum, instruction, and assessment	Providing teams with ready access to information on promising practices in curriculum, instruction, and assessment, and learning with team members as they apply that knowledge
12. Creating processes to provide ongoing monitoring of the school's practices and their effect on student learning	Monitoring the individual and aggregate impact of the efforts of collaborative teams on student achievement, engagement, and perceptions, and providing teams with the tools to monitor their own progress
13. Creating the conditions that optimize school improvement efforts	Using evidence of student learning and positive peer pressure to inspire teachers to explore new practices

Figure 3.3. Integration of leadership responsibilities into PLCs.

Continued on next page →

14. Establishing clear procedures and orderly routines	Establishing clear expectations and protocols for the work of collaborative teams
15. Serving as a spokesperson and advocate for the school and linking staff to external resources	Connecting teams to resources, ideas, and support outside of the school
16. Establishing a positive working relationship with each member of the staff	Using the collaborative team process to increase accessibility to teachers and become more familiar with individual teachers and their concerns
17. Providing teachers with the time, resources, materials, and support to help them succeed at what they are being asked to do	Ensuring that each collaborative team has the necessary time, materials, information, and support to effectively execute their work
18. Recognizing the undercurrents of the informal organization of the school and using that information to be proactive in addressing problems and concerns	Using ongoing discussions with team leaders to discern current or future issues that might affect the functioning of the school
19. Being visible throughout the school and having positive interactions with staff and students	Meeting with each team on at least a quarterly basis and being actively involved in their concerns

The Collaborative Team as a Catalyst for Shared Leadership

A second way in which principals benefit from the collaborative team structure of the PLC process is the opportunity the structure creates for shared leadership. Once again, no single person has all of the knowledge, skills, expertise, and energy to fulfill each of the twenty-one leadership responsibilities. The need for creating a strong leadership team has been cited repeatedly in both educational and organizational research (Elmore, 2003; Kanter, 1999; Kotter, 1996; Marzano et al., 2005; Sergiovanni, 2005). The role of leaders in effective organizations is increasingly focused on enabling people throughout the organization to take the lead in identifying and solving problems (Katzenbach & Kahn, 2010).

Effective principals will not attempt to do it alone. They will foster shared leadership by identifying and developing educators to lead their collaborative teams because without effective leadership at the team level, the collaborative process is likely to drift away from the issues most critical to student learning (Gallimore, Ermeling, Saunders, & Goldenberg, 2009).

There are several factors for principals to consider when selecting team leaders:

1. Their influence with their colleagues—The acceptance or rejection of an idea often depends less on the merits of the idea itself than on the person who is supporting it (Rogers, 2003). In most organizations there are some members who are so highly regarded and respected that their support helps convince others a proposal has merit. The people best suited to leading a team are these "opinion leaders" (Katzenbach & Kahn, 2010; Patterson, Grenny, Maxfield, McMillan, & Switzler, 2008).

2. Their willingness to be a champion of the PLC process— Organizations are most effective when leaders throughout the organization speak with one voice regarding priorities and align their own behaviors with those priorities (Blanchard, 2007). The most effective team leaders demonstrate their belief in the PLC process by modeling their own commitment to a focus on learning, collaboration, collective inquiry, and results orientation.

3. Their sense of self-efficacy and willingness to persist—A recent national survey of teachers revealed they believed the two most important factors for improving student achievement were more funding and better support from parents (Markow & Pieters, 2010). This tendency to look for solutions outside one's own sphere of influence is a major

barrier to improving schools. Effective team leaders do not look out the window waiting for someone else to improve their situation—they look in the mirror. They demonstrate their belief that the collective actions of the members of the team can have a significant, positive impact on results. This belief enables them to rally rather than retreat when faced with setbacks because "they assume that negative events are temporary glitches rather than the permanent state of affairs that pessimists see, and that setbacks are due to specific causes that can be identified and fixed" (Kanter, 2004, p. 357). They stay the course.

4. Their ability to think systematically—The most effective team leaders see the interconnections between the work of their teams and the improvement of their schools and districts (Linden, 2003). Whereas ineffective leaders will view the work of teams as a series of disjointed tasks to be accomplished for a checklist, effective team leaders are able to connect the dots. They bring coherence to the collaborative team process.

Training Team Leaders

Team leaders certainly benefit from ongoing training in certain process skills such as building consensus, facilitating dialogue, collaborative problem solving, conducting effective meetings, and resolving conflict (Linden, 2003). It is also very important, however, that they are taught how to lead their colleagues in the completion of specific and concrete tasks vital to the success of a high-performing team (McDougall, Saunders, & Goldenberg, 2007).

The deepest learning for team leaders occurs when they learn by doing—when they are engaged in real work in the context of their own schools. Therefore, the most effective training occurs "just in time" and is interwoven with rather than separate from the work (O'Neil, 1995; Pfeffer & Sutton, 2000). As one comprehensive review of strategies for leadership development concluded,

"Developmental experiences are likely to have the greatest impact when they can be linked to or embedded in a person's ongoing work. . . . Development today means providing people opportunities to learn from their work rather than taking them away from work to learn" (Hernez-Broome & Hughes, 2004, pp. 25, 27). The best way to train team leaders is to present them with the real-world challenge of leading a team combined with ongoing training and support as they work through that challenge.

To illustrate, imagine a principal attempts to help teams develop a results orientation by asking each team to create a SMART goal that is aligned with school and district goals. The principal must now work with team leaders to determine how to best engage their colleagues in developing such goals. The principal and team leaders could anticipate the kinds of questions their colleagues will generate, questions such as the following:

- Why questions—Why should we create a SMART goal? Can you present any rationale as to why we should engage in this work? Is there evidence that suggests the outcome of this work is desirable, feasible, and more effective than what we have traditionally done?

- What questions—What is the exact meaning of the term *SMART goal*? What resources, tools, templates, materials, and examples can you provide to assist in our work?

- How questions—How do we proceed? How do you propose we do this? Is there a preferred process that will help us create a good SMART goal?

- When questions—When will we find time to do this? When do you expect us to complete the task?

- Guiding questions—Which questions are we attempting to answer by engaging in this task? Which questions will help us stay focused on the right work?

- Quality questions—What criteria should we use to judge the quality of our SMART goal? How will we know our goal is consistent with your expectations?

- Assurance questions—What suggestions can you offer
  to increase the likelihood of our success? What cautions
  can you alert us to? Where do we turn when we struggle?
  (Adapted from DuFour, DuFour, Eaker, & Karhanek, 2010)

By reviewing these questions with team leaders beforehand, by providing those leaders with resources to help address each question, and by having them rehearse the process of taking a team through this dialogue prior to engaging in the work, principals provide team leaders with the tools that enhance their likelihood of success. In supporting those leaders individually and collectively as they work their way through each step of the collective inquiry process, principals also develop the dispersed leadership, common commitments, and collective responsibility essential to sustaining the PLC initiative (National Commission on Teaching and America's Future, 2003).

Principals as Capacity Builders

As mentioned earlier in this chapter, it is almost impossible for a single person to fulfill all of the responsibilities of the principalship. The process of principals devoting their effort and energy into developing team leaders will create new time demands on overburdened school leaders. We are convinced, however, that the time principals devote to building the capacity of teachers to work in collaborative teams is more effective than time spent attempting to supervise individual teachers into better performance through the traditional classroom observation and evaluation process (DuFour & Marzano, 2009).

Assume that a well-intentioned high school principal devotes 150 hours each year to classroom walkthroughs, preobservation conferences, formal observations, postobservation conferences, write-ups, and the individual conversations associated with teacher evaluation. If the principal divides his or her time equally among a staff of fifty teachers, each teacher would have the benefit of three hours of the principal's time annually. What might we expect as a result of this effort?

- The principal will be hard pressed to determine the rigor, relevance, clarity, or even the correctness of the content taught in courses ranging from foreign languages, to advanced calculus, to construction trades.

- The teacher is likely to be found satisfactory, if not exemplary. According to a comprehensive study of teacher evaluation in the United States, districts with a binary evaluation system of either satisfactory or unsatisfactory assigned over 99 percent of their teachers a satisfactory rating. In districts with multiple levels of proficiency, 94 percent of the teachers received the top two ratings, and fewer than one percent were deemed unsatisfactory (Weisberg, Sexton, Mulhern, & Keeling, 2009).

- According to teachers themselves, the process is unlikely to impact their practice. Three of every four teachers feel the evaluation process in their schools is merely a formality that is of little help to them (Duffett, Farkas, Rotherham, & Silva, 2008).

Small wonder that the Teaching Commission (2006) found that teacher evaluation in the United States was "arcane" and "largely ineffective" (p. 16).

Now assume that same principal devoted those 150 hours to working with team leaders and collaborative teams. Those teams meet each week to ensure members are clear regarding the essential objectives for each unit of their course, that each student's progress in achieving those objectives is monitored through an ongoing common formative assessment process developed by the team, and that evidence of student learning is being used to inform and improve their practice. This strategy is far more likely to impact teaching.

A recent study of continuously improving school systems throughout the world found that those systems did not rely on evaluation and performance appraisal to hold teachers accountable. Instead, they created systems to ensure that teachers received ongoing evidence of how their students were learning compared to other similar students. As the researchers concluded, "The focus of these systems was on what students learned, not what teachers taught" (Mourshed et al., 2010, p. 85). But the most powerful form of teacher accountability according to the study "came from peers through collaborative practice. By developing a shared concept of what good practice looks like, and basing it on a fact-based inquiry into what works best to help students learn, teachers hold each other accountable" (p. 85).

Classroom observation of teaching certainly has a place (for example, to assist new teachers or to monitor teachers who have been unable to perform satisfactorily). There are processes that will help improve the principal's effectiveness in classroom observation (see Marzano, Frontier, and Livingston, in press), and principals should develop their ability to use those processes. In chapter 7, we describe a protocol in which teachers themselves engage in classroom observations as part of their collaborative team process to improve their instruction. In general, however, principals should heed Fullan's (2010a) advice and rely far less on individualistic strategies and much more on building collective capacity.

We concur with the conclusion of the recent Wallace Foundation study on school and district leadership, which found that districts should help principals redefine their role and restructure their work schedules in order devote more time to matters related to teaching and learning (Louis et al., 2010). Shifting the focus of principals from supervising individual teachers into better performance to helping build the capacity of educators to work as members of results-oriented collaborative teams is perhaps the most powerful strategy for accomplishing this objective.

Conclusion

The very structure of a PLC works against the isolation of educators in that it demands professional interaction. As we explain in subsequent chapters, interaction between teachers regarding student achievement and the identification of student needs relative to specific academic goals is the starting place for substantive dialogue within collaborative teams. With specific student needs identified, interactions within teams turn to the most appropriate instructional practices to address these needs. Thus, the PLC process becomes a platform for forging professional relationships among teachers and administrators that strikes at the heart of the culture of isolation.

This transformation from a culture of isolation to a culture of collaboration will not occur in a school, however, without the effective leadership of the principal. As McLaughlin and Talbert (2006) concluded, "Principals are in a key strategic position to promote or inhibit the development of a teacher learning community in their school. . . . School administrators set the stage and conditions for starting and sustaining the community development process" (p. 56).

Principals do indeed make a difference in student learning, and the most powerful strategy for having a positive impact on that learning is to facilitate the learning of the educators who serve those students through the PLC process.

{ CHAPTER 4 }

Creating the Collaborative Culture of a Professional Learning Community

Effective leaders with moral purpose don't do it alone. And they don't do it by hiring and supporting "individuals." Instead, they develop and employ the collaborative. . . . The collaborative, sometimes known as professional learning communities, gets these amazing results because not only are leaders being influential, but peers are supporting and pressuring each other to do better.

—Michael Fullan

Katie Haycock (1998) summarizes the research on the impact of the quality of instruction on student achievement in a succinct phrase: "Good teaching matters . . . a lot." She goes on to conclude, "In the hands of our best teachers, the effects of poverty and institutional racism melt away" (p. 11). She is not alone in concluding that the instruction students receive from their classroom teacher is one of the most important variables in determining how much they will achieve. Researchers have repeatedly cited the quality of teaching as the most important factor affecting student learning (Buddin & Zamarro, 2009; Hattie, 2009; Marzano, 2003; Rivkin, Hanushek, & Kain, 2005; Shulman, 1983; Wright, Horn, & Sanders, 1997).

If student learning is linked so directly to the quality of instruction they receive on a day-to-day basis, it would seem to follow that the best way to improve student achievement is to focus on developing the knowledge and skills of individual teachers. Researchers have argued that improving teaching is "the prime factor to produce student achievement gains" (Odden & Wallace, 2003, p. 64), "the only way to improve outcomes" (Barber & Mourshed, 2007, p. 4), and the most powerful strategy for improving schooling (Wright et al., 1997).

Conscientious district and school leaders who read this research can logically conclude that the best way to raise student achievement is by focusing on individual teachers, thereby improving their schools one classroom at a time. For example, they might attempt to supervise and evaluate teachers into better performance, dedicating more and more time to classroom observation in order to provide the individual teacher with feedback on his or her effectiveness. They might create incentives for individual teachers to enhance their skills by attending workshops or graduate courses or by offering them merit pay for improved student performance on high-stakes assessments.

However, if these district and school leaders delve more deeply into the research on improving schools and organizations, they will discover a seemingly contradictory message. This research has concluded that focusing on individual development does not develop the interdependence, collaboration, and collective effort essential to improving results (Carroll, 2009; Kruse et al., 1995; Little, 2006; McCauley & Van Velsor, 2003). In their longitudinal study of restructured schools Newmann and Wehlage (1995) found many schools that had competent individual teachers lacked the organizational capacity to raise student achievement because meeting that challenge "is beyond the skills of individual staff" and requires instead the organization of "human, technical, and social resources into an effective collective effort" (p. 29–30). More recently, Fullan (2010a) has argued emphatically that strategies that focus solely on improving individuals will fail to improve schools because meeting that challenge requires building collective capacity.

This seeming contradiction in research returns us, once again, to the major premise of this book. If schools can only be as good as the professionals within them, and if one of the most important variables in student learning is the quality of instruction students receive each day in their classrooms, substantive school improvement will create the conditions that promote more effective teaching in every classroom. The best way to improve the effectiveness of individual educators is not, however, through individualistic strategies that reinforce educator isolation; "isolation is the enemy of improvement" (Elmore, 2003, p. 67). The far better strategy for improving adult practice is developing the results-oriented collaborative culture of a strong PLC, a culture committed to building the *collective* capacity of a staff to fulfill the purpose and priorities of their school or district. The focus must shift from helping individuals become more effective in their isolated classrooms and schools, to creating a new collaborative culture based on interdependence, shared responsibility, and mutual accountability.

This emphasis on collective capacity does not diminish the significance of the individual educator; rather, it reaffirms that importance by creating conditions that promote the ongoing, job-embedded professional learning vital to the continuous improvement of educators. The quality of the PLC at the school level will determine whether efforts to improve adult practice will impact student achievement in a positive way (Desimone, Porter, Garet, Yoon, & Birman, 2002). Put another way, effective professional development for individual educators will ultimately "be judged by its capacity for building (and building on) professional community" (Little, 2006, p. 2).

Acknowledging the Challenge

The collaborative team is the basic structure of a PLC and the engine that drives continuous improvement. The research supporting both teams and collaboration is extensive. As a recent summary of that research concluded, "Overall, the studies show us that when teachers are given the time and tools to collaborate they become lifelong learners, their instructional practice improves, and they are ultimately able to increase student achievement far beyond what any of them could accomplish alone" (Carroll, Fulton, & Doerr, 2010, p. 10). (For a summary of some of the research on teams and collaboration, visit www.allthingsplc.info.) Conversely, we are not aware of any research that has concluded the best way to help more students learn at higher levels is to have educators work in isolation.

Furthermore, most of the professional organizations that represent teachers and principals have endorsed the premise that educators should work collaboratively. According to a national survey, two-thirds of teachers and 78 percent of principals agree that greater collaboration among educators "would have a major impact on improving student achievement" (Markow & Pieters, 2010, p. 9). Yet despite the widespread evidence of its benefits and the proclaimed support for collaboration, the transformation from a culture in which individual educators work in isolation to one in which they work as members of interdependent collaborative teams remains a formidable challenge.

Consider this analogy: obesity is a problem plaguing a growing number of Americans. The best strategy an individual can use for solving that problem is widely understood—eat less and exercise more. This solution is grounded in research, is universally endorsed by the healthcare industry, and has been proven successful by people throughout the country. Although this most promising strategy is clearly understood and readily acknowledged, it remains challenging to implement. It requires an individual to change long-standing assumptions, expectations, and habits regarding food. It requires the person to relate to food in different ways. And, most importantly, it requires embracing and sustaining an entirely new lifestyle—forever. Pursuing short-term fad diets in spurts won't accomplish the goal of losing weight, keeping it off, and becoming fit. We know all of this to be true; nonetheless, it is difficult to put what we know into practice.

The same can be said of the PLC process with its emphasis on a collaborative culture. There is growing recognition that the process represents a powerful strategy for improving student achievement, but bringing it to life in the real world of schools remains difficult. Educators are asked to change long-standing assumptions, expectations, and habits regarding schooling. They are asked to relate to colleagues and students in new ways. They are called upon to abandon the tradition of pursuing the latest educational fad and instead are asked to sustain a commitment to a very different way of operating schools—forever.

Difficult, but Doable

We offer this caution so that school and district leaders approach the task of implementing the PLC process with a realistic appreciation of the predictable turmoil that lies ahead. The caution is not, however, intended to discourage leaders from assuming the challenge. The task is difficult, but it is doable.

In 1997, Michael Fullan wrote, "It is easy to be pessimistic about educational reform. There are many reasons to be discouraged. From a rational-technical point of view, the conclusion that large-scale school reform is a hopeless proposition seems justified" (p. 216). Nonetheless, he urged educators to cling "to our last virtue: hope" (p. 221). More recently, a decidedly more upbeat Fullan (2010b) asserted that the increasing clarity regarding the precise strategies to improve student learning makes it possible for educators to experience dramatic gains in student achievement in a single year—even in large schools.

We agree that the increasing knowledge base regarding school improvement is cause for optimism. How quickly and successfully that knowledge can be translated into specific and effective actions that impact adult and student learning will depend to a great extent on the skill and persistence of educators themselves. Let's examine some of what we have learned about the precise strategies for building the collaborative culture of a PLC and the common mistakes to avoid.

Reciprocal Accountability: The Key to Building Collective Capacity

The PLC process will require all educators to develop new knowledge, apply new skills, and engage in new practices. Those who lead the process at the district, school, or team level must therefore accept responsibility for providing educators with the clarity, structures, resources, and ongoing support essential to their success. If leaders are going to hold others accountable for improving their performance in some area, then leaders must demonstrate accountability to them by helping develop their capacity to meet the new expectation (Elmore, 2003). In the remainder of this chapter, we offer seven areas district, school, and team leaders must address to help those they serve succeed as members of high-performing collaborative teams.

1. Organize Staff Into Meaningful Teams

Leaders who create artificial teams do great damage to the collaborative culture. When staff select which group they will join based on friendships, when groups are created based on common interests that have little to do with teaching and learning, or when principals create the "leftover team" of singletons who share neither content nor students, they undermine the collaborative team process. A collaborative team is more than a group of random people who meet periodically to see if they can discover a topic of conversation. A collaborative team in a PLC is a group of people working interdependently to achieve a common goal for which members are mutually accountable. *In the absence of interdependence, one or more common goals, and mutual accountability, a group cannot be a team.*

The most important criterion in organizing educators into teams is their shared responsibility for addressing the fundamental questions that drive the work of a PLC (DuFour, DuFour, Eaker, & Many, 2010), the questions we introduced in chapter 1:

- What is it we want our students to know?
- How will we know if they are learning?
- How will we respond when individual students do not learn?
- How will we enrich and extend the learning for students who are proficient?

There are a variety of structures that support meaningful teams as they pursue these questions (see the feature box on page 73, Team Structures). Vertical teams (such as the primary grade teachers or the Spanish language teachers) can work together to create a strong curricular program and strategies for monitoring student progress through the curriculum. Interdisciplinary teams can be effective, but only if they have an overarching academic goal that focuses the team on improved student achievement. Districtwide teams and electronic teams provide ways for teachers in very small schools or teachers of single courses to participate in the collaborative process in a meaningful way.

Specialist teachers can become members of grade-level or course-specific teams that are pursuing outcomes that are logically linked to their areas of expertise. For example, an elementary school physical education teacher can work with a fourth-grade team in teaching percentages as a natural part of his course by asking students to calculate their free-throw percentages or batting averages. A special education teacher can join a content team to help address a history of poor performance in that course by special education students.

The most logical and easiest team structure to establish is the course-specific or grade-level team. Furthermore, these job-alike teams are typically most effective in improving learning for both the adults and students. A recent study found this structure was "critical to teachers sustaining and benefiting from instructional inquiry" (Gallimore et al., 2009). As the researchers found:

> In the framework we investigated, a "learning team"
> . . . is typically composed of three to seven individuals
> teaching the same grade level, course, or subject area.
> . . . In elementary programs, grade-level teams fulfill
> this function. At the secondary level, we have been
> most successful when teachers are organized into
> course-level (or subject area) teams, such as seventh-
> grade pre-algebra, or ninth-grade English. To be suc-
> cessful, teams need to set and share goals to work on
> that are immediately applicable to their classrooms.
> Without such goals, teams will drift toward superficial
> discussions.

Judith Warren Little (2006) came to a similar conclusion, arguing that teachers are more likely to improve their practice when their learning is content based and they work with colleagues to focus on the curriculum, instruction, and assessment linked to their subject. Saphier, King, and D'Auria (2006) concur and contend that while other structures may have their place, the culture of a school, its academic focus, and its professional relationships are revealed by "what happens in teams that share content" (p. 52). Stigler and Hiebert (2009) also found that the best structure to help teachers improve their instruction is grouping teachers in the same content who share the same learning goals for students because "in this environment, different approaches can be planned together, tested in multiple classrooms, and revised based on their students' learning needs" (p. 36). In short, the collective inquiry that drives the work of collaborative teams in a PLC is typically easiest to pursue in job-alike, course-specific, or grade-level specific teams.

Team Structures

- **Same course or grade-level teams** are those in which, for example, all the geometry teachers or all the second-grade teachers in a school form a collaborative team.

- **Vertical teams** link teachers with those who teach content above or below their students.

- **Electronic teams** use technology to create powerful partnerships with colleagues across the district, the state, or the world.

- **Interdisciplinary teams** found in middle schools and small high schools can be an effective structure if members work interdependently to achieve an overarching curricular goal that will result in higher levels of student learning.

- **Logical links** put teachers together in teams that are pursuing outcomes linked to their areas of expertise.

2. Provide Teams With Time to Collaborate

It is perplexing to see the number of districts that proclaim the importance of staff members working collaboratively that provide neither the time nor the structure vital to collaboration. It is disingenuous to assert that working together is an organizational priority and then do nothing to support it. It is equally disingenuous to argue that the funding crisis in American education makes it impossible for districts to provide teachers with time to collaborate when there are many ways to provide that time without increasing costs.

One of the major impediments to providing time for educators to work together is the uniquely American notion that a teacher who is not presenting a lesson in front of a classroom of students is not working. Other nations are not encumbered by this premise. Although the hours in the work week for teachers across countries are comparable, American teachers at all levels spend far more time in the classroom than their international counterparts. American teachers devote an average of 1,072 hours to teaching each year. That represents 36 percent more time in the classroom than the elementary teachers in the thirty nations surveyed by the Organisation for Economic Cooperation and Development and 60 percent more time than upper secondary teachers in those countries (OECD, 2010).

The reason for the huge difference in the amount of time teachers are assigned to the classroom between these nations and the United States can be attributed to one major factor. In those countries, which include countries that have made the greatest progress in educational achievement since 1980, veteran teachers are provided with "15 to 25 hours a week . . . to plan collaboratively and engage in analysis of student learning, lesson study, action research, and observations of one another's classrooms that help them continually improve their practice" (Darling-Hammond, 2010, p. 193). As OECD reports, "In most survey countries there is *regularly scheduled collaboration among teachers on instructional issues* in the vast majority of schools" (2009, p. 85; emphasis in original).

School and district leaders must play a role in changing the perception that teachers engaged in meaningful collaboration are not "working." They can begin this change by actually taking steps to provide teachers with time for collaboration.

Teachers are not blameless in the struggle to ensure they are provided with collaborative time. It is not uncommon for teachers to rail against any schedule that substitutes even one hour of individual planning time for collaborative planning time. We know of no research that has concluded a solitary teacher planning in isolation five hours per week will help students learn at higher levels than one who is allotted only four hours to plan in isolation. Conversely, there is considerable evidence that when teachers work together on the right work, even for as little as one hour each week, we can expect gains in student achievement.

Another common occurrence is for teachers to argue that the district should assume additional costs in order for them to collaborate. They call for substitute teachers to be hired or for teachers to receive additional compensation for working with their colleagues. These proposals are dead on arrival in an era when most districts are struggling to cut budgets rather than add new expenditures. Furthermore, these proposals suggest collaboration is something done in addition to one's work as a teacher rather than as an integral part of contemporary teaching.

Perhaps the most common position for teachers and their representatives to take in regard to collaborative time is that the only possible way to provide that time is to shut down the school during contractual hours and send students home. The National Commission on Time and Learning (1994), a major advocate for teacher collaboration, advised against this strategy, arguing that time for collaboration should not come at the expense of student learning time. Furthermore, we know of districts that have used this strategy to provide time for teachers to work together, only to have the community rise up in opposition, not because teachers were collaborating but because of the inconvenience and hardship it created on families to have their children's weekly schedule disrupted. In the mid-1990s, *Prisoners of Time* (National Education Commission on Time and Learning, 1994) issued the clarion call for providing teachers with time to work together, but if educators contend that the only way they can collaborate is to shut down the school and keep children at home, little will be done to provide that time in the foreseeable future.

So school boards, superintendents, principals, and teachers must work together to provide time for educators to collaborate, but they must also recognize that there are ways to provide that time that will not require the school to be closed, will not cost money, and will not result in a significant loss of instructional time. There are several readily accessible strategies to provide time for teachers to collaborate according to these three criteria. The allthingsplc.info website explains eight of those strategies in considerable detail including:

1. Creating common preparation time

2. Implementing a parallel schedule

3. Adjusting the start and end of the teacher workday

4. Sharing classes

5. Using large group lessons, testing, and assemblies

6. Banking time

7. Devoting time designated for professional development to teams

8. Using faculty meeting time

The same website includes over 150 schools from throughout North America that have created processes to bring educators together to collaborate during their regular contractual day on at least a weekly basis while students are on campus in ways that do not cost money and do not result in significant loss of instructional time. The key here is that the schools did not *find* time for collaboration; they *made* time for collaboration. Until school and district leaders—administrators and teachers—address and resolve the issue of time, their commitment to creating PLCs must be called into question.

3. Provide Supportive Structures That Help Groups Become Teams

In too many cases, school and district leaders are settling for congenial, collegial groups rather than insisting that those groups begin to function as collaborative teams. Certain structures and processes assist in making the transition from groups to teams, and effective leaders will ensure they are in place.

For example, teams are more effective when they have clarified expectations regarding how they will work together, translated those expectations into collective commitments, and use the commitments to monitor their working relationship on an ongoing basis (Garmston & Wellman, 1999; Goleman, Boyatzis, & McKee, 2002; Katzenbach & Smith, 2003; Lencioni, 2005; Patterson et al, 2008). Katzenbach and Smith (2003) write that at the heart of team interaction lies:

A commitment-building process . . . a social contract among its members that relates to their purpose, and guides and obligates how they must work together. . . . At its core, team accountability is about the promises we make to ourselves and others, promises that underpin two critical aspects of teams: commitment and trust. (pp. 59–60)

Although clarifying these commitments does not eliminate the possibility of conflict, it does provide teams with a basis for addressing and resolving the problem (Patterson, Grenny, McMillan, & Switzler, 2002). The clarity regarding what members have committed to do increases the likelihood that they will be able to surface and resolve actions and behaviors that interfere with the likelihood of success (Lencioni, 2003).

Another structure essential to effective teams is the identification of one or more specific goals the team will work to achieve. Once again, we argue that without a common goal that members can achieve only by working together interdependently, a group cannot become a team. Leaders who hope to create high-performing collaborative *teams* must take steps to ensure every team benefits from interdependent relationships and specific performance goals.

Unless a team is pursuing the right kind of goal, however, organizing teachers into teams is unlikely to impact either professional practice or student learning (Elmore, 2003). Because the work of teams should advance the fundamental purpose of the school—high levels of learning for all students—the goals set by each team should be SMART goals as we explained in chapter 1.

The idea that districts, schools, and individuals should have goals is certainly not new. We have witnessed districts devote a great deal of time and energy to creating voluminous lists of goals each year. Very often, those goals focus on projects (we will implement the block schedule), activities (we will train staff in authentic assessment), or tasks to be completed by adults (all teachers will complete a professional growth plan). This kind of goal setting is not what we are referring to here. As one recent study of improving schools concluded, the presence of schoolwide goals does not impact student achievement unless teachers translate those goals into specific goals for their grade-level teams (McDougall et al., 2007). Perhaps that is because "schools" do not have goals. Only people can have goals, and until people within the organization have translated goals into specific performance targets, there is little reason to anticipate improvement.

Therefore, effective SMART goals for teams will focus on concrete evidence of student learning. Achieving the goal may require a multitude of activities, projects, and tasks, but they represent the means to an end, not the end itself. Professional learning communities are fixated on students acquiring the knowledge, skills, and dispositions vital to their success, and therefore SMART goals established by collaborative teams must call both for gathering evidence of student learning and acting on that evidence (Timperley & Alton-Lee, 2008).

The goals should be established *by* the teams, not for the teams, if they are to be *team* goals. The team goal should, however, contribute to and align with school and district goals. Every member should be clear on the goal, how he or she can contribute to its achievement, and the specific indicators the team will use to monitor progress.

The link between collaborative goal setting and improved performance has been well established both in organizational and educational research (Blanchard, 2007; Dolejs, 2006; Gallimore et al., 2009; Lencioni, 2005; O'Hora & Maglieri, 2006; Schmoker, 2006; WestEd, 2000). As one study concluded, "Within teams there is nothing more important than each member's commitment to a common purpose and set of related performance goals for which the group holds itself jointly accountable" (Katzenbach & Smith, 2003, p. 44). Leaders at all levels who hope to develop the capacity of educators to function as members of high-performing teams should ensure every team has the benefit of one or more clearly defined and agreed-upon goals.

4. Clarify the Work Teams Must Accomplish

A skillful manager can assign people into meaningful teams, create schedules that provide them with time to collaborate, and guide teams in creating acceptable norms and SMART goals. It takes effective *leaders,* however, to help teams clarify their purpose and priorities, focus on the right work, and continuously improve their effectiveness.

Perhaps the biggest mistakes leaders make in attempting to create a collaborative culture is to assign teachers or principals into groups and encourage them to collaborate—with little other direction or support. They merely hope for the best. The likelihood that people who have worked in isolation their entire careers will suddenly discover how to work effectively as a team, or will identify the nature of the work they should focus on is extremely remote. Hope may be a virtue, but it is not an effective strategy.

Educators often squander their precious collaborative time on issues that will impact neither professional practice nor student achievement because they are unclear about the nature of the work to be done, a tragedy that occurs often in the name of collaborative teaming. Teachers and principals who collaborate will improve schools only when they are relentlessly focused on student learning (Carroll et al., 2010; Chenoweth, 2009; Hattie, 2009). Collaborating on the wrong work and engaging in collective inquiry into the wrong questions will not have a positive impact on student achievement. If the reason educators are assigned into teams and given time to collaborate is to help students learn at high levels, teams must demonstrate the discipline to focus on those issues that have the most significant impact on student learning.

In *Learning by Doing: A Handbook for Professional Learning Communities at Work,*[TM] Rick and his coauthors provide eighteen critical issues for team consideration that can be a powerful tool in helping provide the appropriate focus (DuFour, DuFour, Eaker, & Many, 2010, pp. 130–131). (Visit **go.solution-tree.com/plcbooks** to download this reproducible.) Each of the issues is linked by research to either gains in student achievement or high-performing teams. If educators concentrate their efforts on these issues, student learning is likely to improve. If they do not demonstrate the discipline to engage in the right work, there is no reason to expect students to benefit.

A five-year study of schools that ultimately demonstrated tremendous gains in student achievement revealed that for two years there was no evidence of improvement despite the fact that teachers had been given time to collaborate. In the third year, the facilitators working with the schools insisted that teams use a recurring cycle of collective inquiry—clarifying what students were to learn, jointly planning instruction to address that learning, implementing their plan as a team, tracking student progress through team-developed common assessments, using the evidence to identify problems in student learning, applying their collective expertise to address the problems, and reflecting on the effectiveness of their solution to determine next steps. This process led to extraordinary gains in achievement in every one of the schools that implemented it. The researchers concluded it is critical that teams utilize a protocol that helps them focus on the right work if the collaborative process is to benefit teachers and students (Gallimore et al., 2009).

One of the more pointless debates going on in many school districts is who will decide how teams will use their collaborative time. Will administrators dictate the nature of the work of teams, or will teachers have control over how they will use this time? The debate is fueled by a question of power, not a question of effectiveness. Districts that hope to promote the PLC process should address this issue by doing what PLCs do when important decisions need to be made—building shared knowledge. Administrators and teachers should work together to identify the "right work" of teams—the work with the greatest potential to have both a positive impact on student learning and the capacity of staff to function as members of high-performing teams.

For example, those who take the time to address this issue on the basis of evidence rather than power will find very little disagreement on the following:

- Teams are more effective when members have clarified their expectations regarding how they will work together, when they have made commitments regarding those expectations, and when they are working interdependently to achieve common SMART goals. Therefore, teams should establish team norms and SMART goals.

- Student learning improves when students have access to a guaranteed and viable curriculum. Therefore, teams should study state standards, district curriculum guides, and high stakes assessments, and engage in conversations with the teachers in the course or grade level above them to identify the knowledge and skills most essential to their students. Each member of the team should be able to answer the question, "What must all students learn as a result of the unit we are about to teach?" Very importantly, individual members must commit to implement the agreed-upon curriculum in their classrooms. Team members should also establish common pacing for each unit that allows sufficient time for the essential skills to be taught to ensure all students have an opportunity to learn.

- Students learn more when they have the prerequisite skills and essential vocabulary that enable them to succeed in achieving the intended outcomes of each unit. Therefore, teams should create common preassessments prior to each unit to identify students who lack the prerequisite skills and knowledge. The team and school should then develop and implement a plan for differentiating instruction to assist those students in acquiring the essential skills before moving forward with new direct instruction.

- Student learning improves when it is monitored on a frequently and timely basis and students are given specific and precise feedback regarding how to improve. Therefore, teams should help members become more effective in gathering evidence of student learning in their classroom each day and should develop frequent common formative assessments to monitor student learning on an ongoing basis as a team. Teams should analyze the results together to identify concepts or skills with which students are struggling, consider reasons why they are struggling, and develop strategies to provide students with specific feedback and ongoing support to advance their learning.

• Student learning improves when their teachers are clear on the criteria they will use in judging the quality of student work and can apply the criteria consistently. Therefore, teams should establish the criteria they will use in assessing student work and practice applying their agreed-upon criteria to samples of student work until team members have established inter-rater reliability.

• Students learn more when teachers examine evidence of student learning collectively and use that evidence to inform and improve their practice. Therefore, each member of the team should examine the results of a variety of indicators of student learning to identify the strengths and weaknesses of his or her teaching and then seek the support of teammates to build on strengths and address weaknesses. Furthermore, the entire team should identify problem areas that require professional development and action research on the part of the team until the problem is solved.

• Students learn more when the school creates systems of intervention to ensure individual students receive additional time and support for learning in way that is timely, directive, precise, and systematic. Therefore, the team should create an ongoing process to identify students who are struggling, and the school should provide those students with timely access to a systematic, multitiered plan of intervention to ensure each receives appropriate support. The plan should also enable the school to address the needs of proficient students who would benefit from curriculum enrichment and or extension.

The point we are making here is that if the decision regarding the work of teams is based on the joint study of evidence regarding the work that has the greatest potential impact on student achievement, administrators and teachers should be able to find common ground. The question of how team time will be spent should be addressed on the basis of impact on student and adult learning, not who wields more power.

We have witnessed districts weaken the collaborative team process by attempting to micromanage every detail of team meetings or using that precious time to address administrivia. We have witnessed teachers argue that their alleged right to determine how, or even if, they will work together supersedes all evidence regarding what is best for student learning. We have witnessed districts eviscerate the power of the process by providing time for teachers to collaborate and being indifferent as to how that time was spent.

Collaboration is morally neutral. It will benefit neither students nor practitioners unless educators demonstrate the discipline to co-labor on the right work. The important question every district, school, and team must address is not, "Do we collaborate?" but rather, "What do we collaborate about?" To paraphrase W. Edwards Deming, it is not enough to work hard; you must clarify the right work, and then work hard. Effective leaders at all levels will ensure there is agreement on the right work.

5. Monitor the Work of Teams and Provide Direction and Support as Needed

The corollary to clarifying the work that must be done in the collaborative team process is developing strategies for monitoring that work. One of those strategies calls upon teams to develop products that flow from the dialogue of a team engaged in collective inquiry on the right work.

At the school level, the Critical Issues for Team Consideration worksheet from *Learning by Doing* (available to download at **go.solution-tree.com/plcbooks**) can again be an important tool to help teachers and principals monitor progress. Each of the eighteen issues should lead to a product that results from the work of the team. Teams will create team norms, SMART goals, lists of essential outcomes for each unit, common assessments, and so on and should submit them to school leaders to demonstrate their work.

When school leaders work with their staffs to create a timeline for anticipated products, it helps teams focus on the work to be done. Teams understand that by a certain date, they are expected to present their list of essential outcomes, first common assessment, first analysis of student results from the assessment, and so on. Administrators and teachers alike must guard against the tendency to view these products as a to-do checklist ("We have created norms. Check. We have written a SMART goal. Check.") The products should serve as primary sources for dialogue among teachers on the team as well as between the team and the principal. For example, we recommend that once each quarter the principal meet with each team to review its collaborative work and offer assistance and support as needed.

Establishing expectations for creating and presenting specific products is an important step in building the capacity of educators to work as members of a collaborative team. When educators understand the tangible work products that must be created as a result of their collaboration, they develop greater clarity regarding the nature of their work. A timeline for presenting completed products is an effective tool for monitoring team progress and promotes regular dialogue between team members and between the team and school leaders. As Katzenbach and Smith (2003) concluded in their comprehensive study of effective teams, "*Without discrete team work-products produced through the joint, real contributions of team members, the promise of incremental or magnified perfor-mance impact goes untapped"* (p. 90, emphasis added).

6. Avoid Shortcuts in the Collaborative Team Process

Every leader who attempts to implement the PLC process at either the school or district level will be encouraged to circumvent the steps in that process. They will be told that teachers in a school have a good working relationship, and so they don't need team norms. Teachers are too busy to collaborate about what students should learn, so simply provide them with state standards and a district curriculum guide and skip the dialogue. Teachers don't have the skills to create good common assessments, so purchase commercial assessments or have the central office staff create benchmark assessments in lieu of teachers working together to gather evidence of student learning. Teachers do not know how to analyze data, so someone else should be hired to do the analysis and report the results. It is the *process* of building shared knowledge and the *collaborative dialogue* about that shared knowledge that builds the capacity of staff to function as high-performing teams. Every time leaders remove teams from that process, they lessen the likelihood of building capacity. Leaders enhance the effectiveness of others when they provide clarity regarding what needs to be done and ongoing support to help staff succeed. They do not develop others by doing the work for them.

7. Celebrate Short-Term Wins, and Confront Those Who Do Not Contribute to Their Teams

Any chapter on how leaders build the capacity of others to work in collaborative teams must address the yin and yang of celebration and confrontation. It is difficult to create momentum for the collaborative team process and impossible to sustain the process without recognizing and celebrating both concerted effort and incremental progress. Effective PLCs weave expressions of appreciation and admiration into the routine life of the school. Conversely, the culture of *defined* autonomy vital to the PLC process depends on leaders who are willing to be direct in addressing those who make no contribution to their collaborative teams. Leaders who are unwilling to confront staff members who ignore the collaborative team process not only undermine that process but also damage their relational trust with the rest of the faculty (Bryk & Schneider, 2004). In fact, Lencioni (2003) advises leaders "who don't have the courage to force team members to step up to the requirements of teamwork" to avoid the collaborative team concept altogether.

Conclusion

Creating the conditions to help others succeed is one of the highest duties of a leader. If school and district leaders are to create the conditions that help more students succeed at learning at higher levels, they must build the capacity of educators to function as members of high-performing collaborative teams. As Fullan (2010b) writes, "Time and again we see the power of collective capacity. When the group is mobilized with focus and specificity, it can accomplish amazing results" (p. 9).

To create the conditions for high-performing collaborative teams, school leaders must develop the clarity of purpose and priorities, structures, support, feedback, and dispersed leadership essential to successful teams. They must be willing to be directive about the work that must be done by teams, but they must also accept the obligation of providing every team with what it needs to succeed in what it is being asked to do.

Thus far, we have focused on how district and school leaders create the conditions to support the collaborative culture of a PLC. In the subsequent chapters, we turn our attention to the specific work that teachers undertake as members of PLCs. Once again, that work will center on four critical questions:

1. What is it we want our students to learn?

2. How will we know if our students are learning?

3. How will we respond when students do not learn?

4. How will we enrich and extend the learning for students who are proficient?

In making this transition, we draw heavily on Bob's lifetime of research into these questions. His work on the first question, "What is it we want our students to learn?" has helped educators around the world recognize the importance of implementing what he has termed a *guaranteed and viable curriculum*, a subject we address in chapter 5. His interest in assessment has established new strategies for gathering and analyzing evidence of student learning, which we present in chapter 6. His ongoing research on effective instruction provides a framework to help teachers and teams respond to the third question by considering more effective instructional strategies when assessment results reveal students are struggling. Chapter 7 presents that research, provides detailed information on how teams can plan for effective instruction based on different learning goals, and offers a process to help teams work collaboratively to assess the impact of their instruction. In chapter 8, we explore the topics of intervention and enrichment, and we conclude with a review of the emotional side of leadership at all levels.

We hope these next chapters illustrate how the PLC process impacts the very heart of the educational enterprise—the classroom.

CHAPTER 5

Developing a Guaranteed and Viable Curriculum

Schools that function as professional learning communities are characterized by academic focus that brings clarity, coherence, and precision to every classroom. These schools have a compact list of clear learning expectations for each grade and subject or course and tangible exemplars of student proficiency for each learning expectation.

—Jonathon Saphier

In *What Works in Schools* (2003), Bob identifies a guaranteed and viable curriculum as the variable most strongly related to student achievement at the school level. That is, one of the most powerful things a school can do to help enhance student achievement is to guarantee that specific content is taught in specific courses and grade levels. This might seem obvious, but in actual practice, few districts and schools can make this guarantee.

The fact that a district creates a curriculum guide and distributes it to teachers does little to guarantee students have access to the same knowledge and skills. Teachers can and do interpret documents differently, assign different levels of priority to recommended content, or simply ignore the documents. In short, it is not unusual to see a huge gap between the *intended* curriculum established by the state or district and the *implemented* curriculum taught when teachers close their classroom doors (Marzano,

2003). As E. D. Hirsch (1996) wrote in *The Schools We Need and Why We Don't Have Them:*

> We know, of course, that there exists no national cur-
> riculum, but we assume, quite reasonably, that agree-
> ment has been reached locally regarding what should
> be taught to children at each grade level—if not within
> the whole district, then certainly within an individual
> school. . . . The idea that there exists a coherent plan
> for teaching content within the local district, or even
> within the individual school, is a gravely misleading
> myth. (p. 26)

Even if teachers are using the same textbook, there is no assurance that students will be taught the same content. As Stevenson
and Stigler (1992) noted in *The Learning Gap:*

> Daunted by the length of most textbooks and know-
> ing that the children's future teachers will be likely to
> return to the material, American teachers often omit
> some topics. Different topics are omitted by different
> teachers thereby making it impossible for the chil-
> dren's later teachers to know what has been covered
> at earlier grades—they cannot be sure what their stu-
> dents know and do not know. (p. 140)

The literature on opportunity to learn (OTL) also highlights the
problems that arise when a school is unable to guarantee that
teachers will address specific content at specific grade levels in
specific courses. The concept of OTL is powerful in its simplicity:
the extent to which students are provided with opportunities to
learn important content is directly related to whether they learn
that content. This rudimentary but powerful fact emerged in the
1960s in international studies of student achievement (see Husen,
1967). Since then, OTL has become an implicit or explicit part of
most—if not all—discussions of school reform.

In a professional learning community, educators are committed to helping students acquire the same essential knowledge and
skills regardless of the teacher to whom they are assigned. Once

again, the first of the big ideas of a PLC is that the staff is committed to helping all students learn, and the first critical question educators in a PLC must consider in addressing that big idea is, "Learn what?" The only way the curriculum in a school can truly be guaranteed is if the teachers themselves, those who are called upon to deliver the curriculum, have worked collaboratively to do the following:

- Study the intended curriculum.

- Agree on priorities within the curriculum.

- Clarify how the curriculum translates into student knowledge and skills.

- Establish general pacing guidelines for delivering the curriculum.

- Commit to one another that they will, in fact, teach the agreed-upon curriculum.

If schools are to establish a truly guaranteed and viable curriculum, those who are called upon to deliver it must have both a common understanding of the curriculum and a commitment to teach it. PLCs monitor this clarity and commitment through the second critical question that teachers in a PLC consider, "How will we know if students are learning?" That question is specifically intended to ensure that the guaranteed curriculum is not only being *taught to* students but, more importantly, is being *learned by* students. In short, the collective inquiry of the collaborative team process in a PLC is purposefully designed to ensure students have access to a guaranteed and viable curriculum.

It is important to note the two parts in the concept of a guaranteed and viable curriculum: The fact that it is *guaranteed* assures us that specific content is taught in specific courses and at specific grade levels, regardless of the teacher to whom a student is assigned. The fact that it is *viable* indicates that there is enough instructional time available to actually teach the content identified as important.

A curriculum cannot be guaranteed unless it is also viable. Again, while this might seem obvious, research over the years has indicated that many school and district curricula do not adhere to the viability criterion. For example, in the late 1990s, when national and state standards reached their full bloom, researchers at Mid-continent Research for Education and Learning (McREL) estimated that the national standards in fourteen subject areas required 71 percent more time to teach than was actually available (see Marzano, Kendall, & Cicchinelli, 1998; Marzano, Kendall, & Gaddy, 1999). Since that time, some progress has been made on lessening the amount of content identified in the national and state standards. One high-profile effort to this end is the Common Core of Knowledge project, which proposes to develop standards that are used by multiple states. This has some obvious advantages over each state continuing to develop and revise its own unique standards, not the least of which is the money required every time a state changes or updates its standards. With a common set in place, standards need be updated only once for all states adopting the common core.

As useful as this project has been, it still exhibits some of the same old problems for schools and districts wishing to construct a viable curriculum in the context of a PLC. Consider the following fourth-grade English language arts standard from the Common Core State Standards (2010, p. 28). A student will:

> Demonstrate command of the conventions of standard English grammar and usage when writing or speaking:
>
> a. Use relative pronouns (who, whose, whom, which, that) and relative adverbs (where, when, why).
>
> b. Form and use the progressive (e.g., *I was walking; I am walking; I will be walking*) verb forms.
>
> c. Use modal auxiliaries (e.g. *can, may must*) to convey various conditions.

    d. Order adjectives within sentences according to conventional patterns (e.g., *a small red bag* rather than *a red small bag*).

    e. Form and use prepositional phrases.

    f. Produce complete sentences, recognizing and correcting inappropriate fragments and run-ons.

    g. Correctly use frequently confused words (e.g. *to, too, two; there, their*).

Even a cursory analysis of this standard reveals that it contains multiple elements that are difficult to assess when considered as a set, particularly in the context of the writing and speaking generated by students. (In chapter 6, we consider in depth the problem of assessing too many elements in a single test.) The issue of standards with multiple elements is put in sharp focus when one considers the number of standards included in the common core. At the fourth-grade level alone the common core includes forty-three standards, many of which are like the previous example. When one considers the fact that a busy fourth-grade teacher has only thirty-six weeks and 180 days in the school year, the task of teaching forty-three standards appears daunting if not impossible.

In short, while well intended and certainly a step in the right direction, the common core standards have not solved the problem for the classroom teacher of developing standards that truly represent a viable curriculum—one that can be adequately addressed in the current time available to classroom teachers.

PLCs and a Guaranteed and Viable Curriculum

A guaranteed and viable curriculum is a basic tenet of the PLC process. In chapter 1, we clarified that the first of the three big ideas that drive the PLC process is that the fundamental purpose of the school is to ensure that all students learn at high levels. In order to fulfill that purpose, educators must be clear on the knowledge, skills, and dispositions all students must acquire. The process to establish this clarity is specifically intended to address the principle of a guaranteed and viable curriculum. When done well, it ensures that specific content will be taught in specific courses and at specific grade levels regardless of the teacher to whom a student is assigned.

A guaranteed and viable curriculum is also highly compatible with the third big idea of the PLC process. In order to know if students are learning and to respond appropriately to their needs, educators must create a results orientation. SMART goals are vital to bringing this principle to life. When structured in specific ways, a guaranteed and viable curriculum can greatly enhance the design of SMART goals. We discuss this in chapter 6.

Finally, the concept of a guaranteed and viable curriculum is vital to the concept of teachers as leaders. Clarity regarding intended outcomes is a fundamental element of effective leadership (Buckingham, 2005; Drucker, 1992). Effective leaders know what they want to accomplish. One of the main differences between effective and ineffective teachers is that effective teachers know "the learning intentions and success criteria of their lessons" (Hattie, 2009, p. 239), and thus are in a position to continuously monitor the progress of their students toward those intended outcomes. When collaborative teams work together to create a guaranteed and viable curriculum, each member of the team has the benefit of a key precondition for effective leadership: clarity regarding what is to be accomplished.

The process of creating a guaranteed and viable curriculum within the context of a PLC should involve a number of considerations including the following: identifying the nature of objectives, identifying the appropriate grain size for objectives, identifying the appropriate number of objectives, articulating levels of knowledge, and designing proficiency scales.

Identifying the Nature of Objectives

The process of creating a guaranteed and viable curriculum begins with identification of content that is considered essential to a course or subject area within a grade level. Educators, even those within PLCs, often use a variety of terms when referring to "critical content." Specifically, terms like *goals, learning goals, objectives, educational objectives, instructional objectives, learning targets, essential elements*, and the like are frequently used to mean the same thing. The term a school or district uses is not important; however, as we mentioned in chapter 2, it is important that educators in a particular school or district develop a common language and shared understanding of the key terms they use. To promote that common language, in this book, we tend to use the term *objective* when referring to content identified as essential for all students to learn. We should note that in other works, Bob (Marzano, 2009a) has used the term *goals*, and Rick DuFour et al. (2010) have used the term *essential learnings* to refer to what we are calling *objectives* in this text. It is instructive to consider briefly the etymology of terms simply to understand the diversity of ways in which they are used.

In the first half of the 21st century, Ralph Tyler (1949a, 1949b) brought the importance of objectives to the attention of educators. Tyler's main message was that educators should construct objectives that provide clear reference to knowledge students were expected to acquire. Prior to Tyler's comments, educators typically identified general categories of knowledge as targets of instruction, such as weather or World War I. Tyler affirmed that much more specificity was required. Krathwohl and Payne (1971) furthered the discussion by making distinctions between three levels or types of objectives: global objectives, instructional objectives, and educational objectives. As described by Marzano & Kendall (2007), global objectives are the most general, representing broad areas of content. For example, "Students will be able to apply basic principles of effective writing." Instructional objectives (sometimes referred to as behavioral objectives) are the most specific of the three types. In his book *Preparing Instructional Objectives,* Robert Mager (1962, p. 21) identified three elements to an effective instructional objective:

1. Performance—An objective always says what a learner is expected to be able to do; the objective

sometimes describes the product or result of the doing.

2. Conditions—An objective always describes the important conditions (if any) under which the performance is to occur.

3. Criterion—Whenever possible, an objective describes the criterion of acceptable performance by describing how well the learner must perform in order to be considered acceptable.

To illustrate, the following is an instructional objective as described by Mager:

Students will be able to solve ten problems regarding two-column addition (performance) at an 80 percent success rate or greater (criterion) in ten minutes or less without the use of a calculator (condition).

Educational objectives are in the middle in terms of level of specificity (Anderson et al., 2001). Like instructional objectives, they identify specific performances (albeit not as specific as Mager's notion of a performance), but they do not identify specific conditions or criteria. The following is an educational objective:

Students will be able to perform two-column addition without any serious errors or omissions.

We recommend that collaborative teams in PLCs use the educational-objective level as the general format for identifying critical content. As they specify the knowledge and skills all students should acquire, they should state that expectation in the form of objectives, much like the two-column addition example that fits Mager's description.

Identifying the Appropriate Grain Size of Objectives

One of the more important aspects for collaborative teams to consider when articulating objectives is the "grain size" at which they are written. *Grain size* refers to how much or how little information and skill is included in the statement of the objective. As Popham (2009b) explains:

> The grain size of an instructional objective refers to the breadth of the outcome teachers seek from students. An example of large grain size would be when a student can generate an original, effective, persuasive essay. That's a significant instructional outcome, and it might take a full semester of school for students to accomplish it. An objective with a small grain size might deal with a less demanding outcome, such [as] being able to correctly spell all the words in a set of thirty "spelling demons." Objectives with small grain size might be achieved in a single class period. (p. 16)

Popham emphasizes the fact that the grain size for objectives should not be too small and uses the spelling example to dramatize his concern. He explains, "During the sixties, advocates of behavioral objectives ended up recommending so many small-grained objectives that we overwhelmed the nation's educators. It was a profound error" (p. 16).

To create objectives at the level appropriate for planning instruction, developing assessments in the classroom, and providing feedback to students, teachers working in collaborative teams in PLCs must consider the type of content to which the objective relates. In general, classroom content fits into one of three general types of knowledge: information, mental procedures, and psychomotor procedures. Table 5.1 on page 98 compares these three types of knowledge. Each of the three types contains two major categories and one or more subcategories. See Marzano and Kendall (2007, 2008) for a detailed description of the three types of knowledge.

Table 5.1: Three Types of Knowledge

Type of Knowledge	Major Categories	Subcategories
Information	Organizing ideas	Principles
		Generalizations
	Details	Time sequences
		Facts
		Vocabulary terms
Mental procedures	Processes	Macroprocedures
	Skills	Tactics
		Algorithms
		Single rules
Psychomotor procedures	Processes	Complex combination procedures
	Skills	Simple combination procedures
		Foundation procedures

Information, technically known as declarative knowledge, includes the major categories of (1) organizing ideas and (2) details. The category of organizing ideas includes principles and generalizations. Details include time sequences, facts, and vocabulary terms. These five subcategories are described in more detail in figure 5.1 on pages 99–101.

Following Popham's rule that objectives should not be too specific but specific enough to provide clear guidance to teachers, we recommend that objectives for informational knowledge be articulated at the organizing-idea level. Specifically, objectives regarding information should usually be stated as generalizations or principles like the following:

> Students will be able to explain specific conditions that put people at risk for substance abuse.

Organizing Ideas
Principles: There are specific types of generalizations that deal with relationships. In general, there are two types of principles in school-related declarative knowledge: cause-effect principles and correlational principles.
Cause-effect principles: These articulate causal relationships. For example, "Tuberculosis is caused by the tubercle bacillus," is a cause-effect principle. Understanding a cause-effect principle involves knowledge of the specific elements within the system and the exact relationships those elements have to one another. That is, to understand the cause-effect principle regarding tuberculosis and the bacterium, one would have to understand the sequence of events that occur, the elements involved, and the type and strength of the relationships between those elements. Understanding a cause-effect principle involves a great deal of information.
Correlational principles: These describe relationships that are not necessarily causal in nature but in which a change in one factor is associated with a change in another factor. For example, "The increase in lung cancer among women is directly proportional to the increase in the number of women who smoke" is a correlational principle. To understand this principle, a student would have to know the specific details about the relationship, including the general pattern of the relationship; that is, the number of women who have lung cancer changes at the same rate as the changes in the number of women who smoke.
These two types of principles are sometimes confused with time sequences that involve cause-effect relationships. A cause-effect sequence applies to a specific situation, whereas a principle applies to many situations. The causes of the Civil War taken together represent a time sequence with some causal relationships. They apply to the Civil War only. However, the cause-effect principle linking tuberculosis and the tubercle bacillus can be applied to many different situations and many different people. Physicians use this principle to make judgments about a variety of situations and a variety of people. The key distinction between principles and cause-effect sequences is that principles can be exemplified in a number of situations, whereas cause-effect sequences cannot; they apply to a single situation only.

Figure 5.1: Examples of informational knowledge.

Continued on next page →

Generalizations: These are statements for which one can provide examples. For instance, "U.S. presidents often come from families that have great wealth or influence" is a generalization for which we can provide examples. It is easy to confuse some generalizations with some facts. Facts identify characteristics of specific persons, places, living and nonliving things, and events, whereas generalizations identify characteristics about classes or categories of persons, places, living and nonliving things, and events. For example, the statement "My dog, Tuffy, is a golden retriever" is a fact. However, the statement "Golden retrievers are good hunters" is a generalization. In addition, generalizations identify characteristics about abstractions. Specifically, information about abstractions is always stated in the form of generalizations. Following are some examples of the various types of generalizations:

- Characteristics of classes of persons (for example, "It takes at least two years of training to become a fireman.")

- Characteristics of classes of places (for example, "Large cities have high crime rates.")

- Characteristics of classes of living and nonliving things (for example, "Firearms are the subject of great debate.")

- Characteristics of classes of events (for example, "The Super Bowl is a premier sporting event each year.")

- Characteristics of abstractions (for example, "Love is one of the most powerful human emotions.")

Details

Time sequences: These are important events that occurred between two points in time. For example, the events that occurred between President Kennedy's assassination on November 22, 1963, and his burial on November 25, 1963, are organized as a time sequence in most people's memories. First one thing happened, then another, then another. Time sequences can include some elements that have a causal relationship.

Facts: Facts are a very specific type of information. They convey information about specific persons, places, living and nonliving things, and events. They commonly articulate information such as the following:

- Characteristics of a specific real or fictitious person (for example, "The fictitious character Robin Hood first appeared in English literature in the early 1800s.")
- Characteristics of a specific place (for example, "Denver is in the state of Colorado.")
- Characteristics of specific living and nonliving things (for example, "The Empire State Building is over 100 stories high.")
- Characteristics of a specific event (for example, "Construction began on the Leaning Tower of Pisa in 1174.")

Vocabulary terms: These are the most specific level of information knowledge. In this system, knowing a vocabulary term means understanding the meaning of a word in a general way. For example, when a student understands declarative knowledge at the level of a vocabulary term, he or she has a general idea what the word means and no serious misconceptions about its meaning. To organize classroom content as vocabulary terms is to organize it as independent words and phrases. The expectation is that students have an accurate but somewhat surface-level understanding of the meaning of these terms.

Source: Adapted from Marzano and Kendall (2007).

The example of a generalization about substance abuse on page 98 is from the subject area of health. There are certainly details related to this generalization, such as the various types of drugs that are commonly misused by students; however, writing objectives at the level of details for informational knowledge would likely result in an overabundance of objectives for every grade level. Thus, we recommend against using that level of detail.

The second type of knowledge in table 5.1 is mental procedures. The two major categories within this type of knowledge are processes and skills. Figure 5.2 (page 102) describes the various types of mental procedures in some depth.

Processes
Macroprocedures: The prefix *macro* indicates that a procedure is highly complex with many subcomponents that require some form of management. Examples include reading and synthesizing a chapter in a book; designing a new system for searching information on the Internet and then storing that information in a common database organized into multiple overlapping categories; and writing a research paper on a specific topic. Typically there are many different ways to successfully execute a macroprocedure. Macroprocedures commonly include tactics, algorithms, and single rules.
Skills
Tactics: A tactic is more commonly referred to as a strategy—a general approach to performing a mental procedure. Tactics are not nearly as complex as macroprocedures. They involve a series of steps that are not performed in a rigid order. For example, the tactic for reading a bar graph has steps that include reading the title, identifying the variable in the vertical axis, identifying the variable in the horizontal axis, determining the metric of the vertical and horizontal axes, and so on. However, these steps do not have to be executed in a specific order for the tactic to be effective.
Algorithms: Algorithms are mental procedures that normally do not vary in application once learned. They have very specific outcomes and very specific steps. For example, multicolumn subtraction and multicolumn addition are algorithms. Once a student solidifies a set of steps, he or she will execute those steps in the same fashion and order every time.
Single rules: The simplest type of mental procedure is a single rule or small set of single rules with no accompanying steps. Single-rule mental procedures are commonly employed in sets. For example, a student who knows three rules for subject-verb agreement within sentences and clear reference between sentences might apply these rules when editing a composition.

Figure 5.2: Examples of mental procedures.

A mental process is the nontechnical name for what is referred to as a macroprocedure. As indicated in table 5.1, there are no subcategories for macroprocedures. The defining characteristics of a mental process is that it contains many interacting components and is quite complex in nature. For example, writing is a macro-procedure that includes many skills, such as tactics for editing for overall logic and for creating transitions between paragraphs. It also includes a wide variety of single-rule procedures, such as capitalizing the first word in a sentence, indenting each paragraph, placing an appropriate punctuation mark at the end of each sentence, and so on.

When articulating objectives for specific units of instruction, it is generally not advisable to focus on a macroprocedure as a whole, simply because it involves so many interacting components. For example, the following is an objective that focuses on the macroprocedure of writing:

> Students will be able to write an effective persuasive essay on a topic of their choice.

While this statement is a good candidate for an end-of-course objective, it is too broad for a particular instructional unit because it does not articulate which of the important components of writing the unit will address. A student might generate good transitions between paragraphs (a component of the writing process) but not employ good descriptive word choice (another component of the writing process). Consequently, when designing unit objectives for mental procedures, collaborative teams should focus on specific tactics. The objective for one unit might be, "Students will be able to establish a central idea." The next unit might call upon students to add descriptive details to support their central idea. A third unit might ask students to demonstrate that they are able to edit their persuasive compositions for transitions between paragraphs. The successful attainment of these unit objectives, over the course of time, should lead students to achieve the macroprocedure—writing a good persuasive essay. We explore this idea in more detail later in this chapter in the section on addressing topics.

Whereas tactics are good candidates for mental-procedure objectives, single rules are not. For example, it would be counterproductive to generate objectives for specific rules regarding punctuation.

The third major type of knowledge identified in table 5.1 (page 98) is psychomotor procedures. This knowledge is organized into two general categories: processes and skills. Figure 5.3 describes the various types of psychomotor procedures in some depth.

Processes
Complex combination procedures: Like macroprocedures, they include a variety of skills interacting in a cohesive manner to accomplish a specific goal. For example, skiing down an expert slope is a complex combination procedure. The skier must execute different types of turns while monitoring and controlling his or her speed, all while employing foundational procedures such as keeping one's balance, shifting one's weight, and so on.
Skills
Simple combination procedures: These are usually the working parts of complex combination procedures. For example, the complex combination procedure of skiing down an expert slope is made up of a set of simple combination procedures such as gradual left and right turns, sharp left and right turns, jump turns left and right, jumps over obstacles, and so on. Each of these are independent to a certain extent in that they serve a unique function and have specific techniques associated with them. However, when used within complex combination procedures, they are all executed as part of a whole that must be managed moment by moment wherein the appropriate or necessary action must be taken at a specific moment in time.
Foundational procedures: These are the most basic type of psychomotor skill. These are procedures commonly used in everyday movement. They include elements like arm-hand steadiness, manual dexterity, eye-hand coordination, speed of limb movement, and so on. While these elements do not typically have to be taught, they commonly must be executed with exceptional precision and/or speed if the simple combination procedures that they make up are to be executed effectively.

Figure 5.3: Examples of psychomotor procedures.

As is the case with mental processes, psychomotor processes have no subcategories. Psychomotor processes are technically referred to as *complex combination procedures*. Like macroprocedures for mental processes, they contain many interacting components. Examples of psychomotor processes include playing defense in basketball or putting together a specific set of moves to create a dance sequence. Skills include simple combination procedures and foundational procedures. For example, a simple combination procedure when playing defense in basketball would be lateral movement from side to side with feet kept wide apart, one hand held high to guard against an opponent's shots and the other hand held low to guard against an opponent's dribble. Foundational procedures are very basic movements used when performing simple combination procedures, such as shuffling across the floor laterally while keeping the feet wide apart or keeping one's hands raised.

As is the case with mental procedures, objectives for psychomotor procedures should not be written at the level of complex combination procedures simply because they are too broad. For example, writing an objective that students will be able to play defense effectively in basketball is probably too broad. A student might be very good at the necessary type of lateral movement, but he or she might be very poor at moving through blocks imposed by the offensive team. The best candidates for objectives are simple combination procedures. For example, a physical education teacher might establish the following objective:

> Students will exhibit effective lateral movement when guarding an opponent in basketball.

Writing objectives at the level of foundational procedures, such as raising and lowering of the hands, would obviously generate far too many detailed objectives.

Identifying the Appropriate Number of Objectives

The first step for a collaborative team in a PLC hoping to generate a guaranteed and viable curriculum is to identify a viable set of objectives. Of course, defining exactly what constitutes a viable set is a critical aspect of this process. One can infer from Popham's comments about objectives that he might recommend only two or three objectives for a given quarter and ten or fewer for an entire year. This is certainly a defensible position. In such cases, members of a collaborative team would focus on those aspects of content for which students are experiencing the most difficulty. Teams might determine areas of need by examining state assessments, benchmark assessments, and even common assessments.

In general, we believe that Popham's comments represent sage advice, particularly in the early stages of collaborative teamwork on curriculum. The initial efforts of a PLC to create a guaranteed and viable curriculum are probably best served if collaborative teams start with relatively few objectives. However, once teachers become accustomed to designing and assessing objectives as described in this chapter and in chapter 6, they should progress to articulating all the objectives for a specific course or the subject-matter content for a particular grade level. For example, figure 5.4 shows objectives for an entire year for eighth-grade science.

Note that in figure 5.4, objectives are organized under topics. For example, objectives 1 and 2 are organized under the topic of "Atmospheric Processes and the Water Cycle," and objectives 3, 4, and 5 are organized under the topic of "Composition and the Structure of the Earth." Additionally, topics are organized under strands. For example, the topics "Atmospheric Processes and the Water Cycle" and "Composition and the Structure of the Earth" are organized under the strand "Earth and Space Sciences" along with the topic "Composition and Structure of the Universe and the Earth's Place in It." Ultimately, the complete articulation of a guaranteed and viable curriculum would result in a set of objectives organized in a way that informs instruction and assessment, like those in figure 5.4.

Strand 1: Earth and Space Sciences
Atmospheric Processes and the Water Cycle   Objective 1: Students will illustrate how climate patterns are affected by the water cycle and its processes.   Objective 2: Students will model how all levels of the earth's atmosphere (troposphere, stratosphere, mesosphere, and thermosphere) are affected by temperature and pressure.
Composition and Structure of the Earth   Objective 3: Students will describe the unique composition of each of the earth's layers and how the earth is affected by the interaction of those layers.   Objective 4: Students will describe the constructive and destructive forces that create and shape landforms.   Objective 5: Students will illustrate each stage of the rock cycle (transitions to igneous, metamorphic, and sedimentary rock).
Composition and Structure of the Universe and the Earth's Place In It   Objective 6: Students will find errors in explanations of how phenomena such as the day, the year, the moon phases, solar and lunar eclipses, tides, and shadows are created and changed by the orbits of the earth and the moon.   Objective 7: Students will list the defining characteristics of each planet in the solar system and make basic comparisons between them.   Objective 8: Students will model how the sun and the planets in our solar system interact.   Objective 9: Students will explain the unique nature and defining elements of different celestial objects.
Strand 2: Life Sciences
Principles of Heredity and Related Concepts   Objective 10: Students will classify specific reproductive characteristics (physical processes, heritable traits, and mutation risks) as either sexual or asexual.   Objective 11: Students will illustrate different ways organisms can be affected by heritable traits (diseases, inherited physical abilities, and appearances).

Figure 5.4: Eighth-grade science objectives.

Continued on next page →

Structure and Function of Cells and Organisms

Objective 12: Students will match specific processes of cell division and differentiation to the correct prokaryotic or eukaryotic organism.

Objective 13: Students will classify cells according to purpose in given multicellular organisms.

Objective 14: Students will describe how cells, tissues, organs, and organ systems create interactive levels of organization.

Objective 15: Students will describe the cause-effect relationships between humans and ecosystems.

Objective 16: Students will explain how food chains and webs work, as well as their places in an ecosystem.

Objective 17: Students will illustrate how ecosystems transform matter in cycles.

Biological Evolution and the Diversity of Life

Objective 18: Students will describe the key components of different theories on how life is thought to have begun and the different implications of those theories on current events and daily life.

Objective 19: Students will explain how natural selection promotes unity and how it promotes diversity.

Strand 3: Physical Sciences

Structures and Properties of Matter

Objective 20: Students will describe the unique elements of isolated, closed, and open thermodynamic systems and make basic comparisons between them.

Objective 21: Students will describe the characteristics of different states of matter.

Objective 22: When given the composition, atomic number, melting point, and boiling point of an element, the student will name and classify it.

Sources of Properties of Energy

Objective 23: Students will classify a given energy as gravitational, chemical, mechanical, or nuclear.

Objective 24: Students will find errors in statements about the defining characteristics of motion, radiant, and thermal energies and sound.

Objective 25: Students will describe the defining characteristics of geothermal, hydropower, wind, solar, ocean, and hydrogen energies and what makes them renewable.
Forces and Motion
Objective 26: Students will explain how factors such as force and friction can affect the motion of an object.
Objective 27: Students will describe the relationship between electricity and magnetism.
Objective 28: Students will explain how mass and distance affect gravitational force.
Strand 4: Nature of Science
Nature of Scientific Inquiry
Objective 29: Students will design and conduct multiple experiments that focus on replication.
Scientific Enterprise
Objective 30: Students will match specific scientific advancements with the scientist who made the discovery.
Objective 31: Students will explain how the scientific enterprise can raise ethical issues and understand what those issues are.

Source: Adapted from Marzano (2009a, pp. 80–81).

Topics as the Ultimate Focus With Procedural Knowledge

In figure 5.4, the topics under which objectives are classified are broad themes. Typically the topics for information content are simply organizational tools. For example, consider the topic "Structure and Function of Cells and Organisms." It includes six objectives:

- Objective 12: Students will match specific processes of cell division and differentiation to the correct prokaryotic or eukaryotic organism.

- Objective 13: Students will classify cells according to purpose in given multicellular organisms.

- Objective 14: Students will describe how cells, tissues, organs, and organ systems create interactive levels of organization.

- Objective 15: Students will describe the cause-effect relationships between humans and ecosystems.

- Objective 16: Students will explain how food chains and webs work, as well as their places in an ecosystem.

- Objective 17: Students will illustrate how ecosystems transform matter in cycles.

These six objectives are certainly related to the overall topic, but not in any dependent way. Rather, mastering these six objectives represents an understanding of six relatively circumscribed knowledge schemas. In contrast, when dealing with mental or psychomotor procedures, it is common for topics to represent much more tightly coupled sets.

For example, assume that a particular grade level has identified the following language arts topic: "Writing Effective Expository Essays." As we saw in the previous discussion, writing an expository essay can be considered a macroprocedure. We also saw that macroprocedures (for mental procedures) and complex combination procedures (for psychomotor procedures) do not make for effective unit objectives because they are too broad and do not allow for specific feedback to students. Macroprocedures and complex combination procedures do, however, make for excellent topics under which to articulate more specific procedural objectives. To illustrate, under the general topic (macroprocedure) of "Writing Effective Expository Essays," a collaborative team might identify the following more specific objectives:

- Students will include in their expository essays a clear thesis statement accompanied by support and qualifiers that limit the scope of their claims.

- Students will include in their expository essays clear transitions between paragraphs and sections.

- Students will include in their expository essays clear reference regarding subject/verb agreement and clear reference for pronouns.

- Students will include in their expository essays word choices that are not redundant but communicate a clear message.

- Students will include in their expository essays beginning-of-sentence capitalization and end-of-sentence punctuation that is appropriate to the essay.

These objectives are all at the skill level. By organizing them under the topic of "Writing Effective Expository Essays," the team communicates to students that, at this particular grade level, mastery of these five skills is what constitutes the broader process of writing effective expository essays. From the beginning, the focus in class would always be on mastering the overall process, even though the emphasis for specific lessons or a specific unit might be on one objective only. The ultimate goal would be for all students to use all five skills articulated in the objectives in concert to generate effective expository essays.

Articulating Levels of Knowledge

Once collaborative teams have identified objectives, the next step is to articulate levels of knowledge for each objective. The reason for this step is grounded in the burgeoning work on learning progressions.

Learning progressions (also known as *learning sequences* and *learning hierarchies*) are attempts to organize academic content into a progression of increasingly more complex and generalizable knowledge. Ideally, each element in a learning progression is necessary to understand the next element or a natural developmental stage of understanding subsequent to the next level. Teachers and PLC teams who establish this clear progression are, once again, modeling effective leadership. Like all great leaders, they "know the importance of breaking mastery into clear, specific, and achievable mini-goals. They take complex tasks and turn them into simple steps, long tasks and make them short, vague tasks and make them specific" (Patterson et al., 2008, p. 124).

Of course there have been attempts to organize curriculum in a sequential manner. For example, in the 1960s science curricula were organized as a sequence of process skills based on the conceptual framework of Gagne. As described by Duschl, Schweingruber, & Shouse (2007):

> These proposed "learning hierarchies" focused on building competence with domain-general processes rather than helping children build frameworks of interrelated science concepts. They had an appeal to teachers and curriculum developers because they broke complex tasks down into simpler elements, identified 14 basic process skills that were proposed to develop in a certain sequence and to underlie scientific thinking, and provided many specific exercises for children to practice these skills. But because they ignored the crucial role of meaning, content, and context and treated science instead as a series of disembodied "skills," they were often carried out as meaningless procedures. (p. 215)

Duschl, Schweingruber, and Shouse go on to say:

> Although Gagne's original formulation of science as a collection of content-free processes has largely been rejected by science educators, its legacy persists both in policy and practice. Many textbooks and curriculum documents still have separate sections on scientific inquiry, science processes, or "the scientific method." Many classroom teachers follow the lead of these resources, teaching skills and inquiry techniques separately from the conceptual content of their courses. (p. 216).

In effect, Duschl and colleagues remind us that just because content is organized in a sequential fashion does not necessarily mean it represents a true progression of knowledge.

Virtually all of the current work on learning progressions assumes that learning complex knowledge for any single dimension involves moving through basic content to more complex content. To illustrate, Joan Herman and Kilchan Choi (2008) describe a fairly detailed learning progression on the topic of buoyancy. They identify the following levels (from highest to lowest) of understanding:

- Student knows that floating depends on having less density than the medium.

- Student knows that floating depends on having a small density.

- Student knows that floating depends on having a small mass and a large volume.

- Student knows that floating depends on having a small mass, or that floating depends on having a large volume.

- Student thinks that floating depends on having a small size, heft, or amount, or that it depends on being made out of a particular material.

- Student thinks that floating depends on being flat, hollow, filled with air, or having holes.

If a student has substantive background knowledge about the topic of buoyancy, a teacher might skip or abbreviate some elements of this sequence. If a student has very little background knowledge about the topic of buoyancy, teachers might articulate certain elements of this progression in even more detail.

Certainly the goal of curriculum developers in various subject areas should be to develop learning progressions for their content. At some point in the future, this will be accomplished when learning progressions are articulated for every topic, in every subject area, at every grade level. In the interim, though, Marzano (2009a, 2010b) has suggested that three levels of proficiency can suffice to provide teachers and students with clear guidance regarding instruction and assessment. These three levels can be readily placed into a rubric or proficiency scale.

The process of constructing proficiency scales begins by identifying content simpler than or subordinate to a given objective as well as content more complex than or superordinate to a given objective. Consider the following science objective designed by a collaborative team of second-grade teachers:

> Students will be able to describe and exemplify what different plants and animals need to survive.

This is informational knowledge at the level of an organizing idea. Next, the collaborative team articulates content that is simpler than or subordinate to the objective, such as:

- Students will be able to recall specific terminology such as *plant, animal, survival.*

- Students will be able to recall details about survival such as the following: Both plants and animals need food, air, and water to survive. Plants absorb nutrients and air through their roots and leaves. Animals use respiration (lungs) to breathe and digestion to process nutrients.

This information is at the detail level. Finally, the collaborative team articulates more complex or superordinate content to the objective, such as:

> Students will be able to compare and contrast different ways in which plants and animals breathe and find nourishment (for example, comparing and contrasting the fact that plants use their roots and leaves to take in air and food, while animals use their lungs to breathe air and their digestive systems to obtain nourishment).

Once collaborative teams identify objectives and their related subordinate and superordinate content, they can easily construct proficiency scales.

Designing Proficiency Scales

The proficiency scales we recommend (Marzano, 2009a, 2010b) have the generic format depicted in figure 5.5.

Score 4.0	More complex content
Score 3.5	In addition to score 3.0 performance, partial success at score 4.0 content
Score 3.0	Target objective
Score 2.5	No major errors or omissions regarding score 2.0 content, and partial success at score 3.0 content
Score 2.0	Simpler content
Score 1.5	Partial success at score 2.0 content, but major errors or omissions regarding score 3.0 content
Score 1.0	With help, partial success at score 2.0 content and score 3.0 content
Score 0.5	With help, partial success at score 2.0 content, but not at score 3.0 content
Score 0.0	Even with help, no success

Copyright Robert J. Marzano

Figure 5.5: Generic form for proficiency scales.

To understand the proficiency scale in figure 5.5, first consider the score 3.0. It involves the target objective identified by a collaborative team. Using the previous example, score 3.0 on the proficiency scale would contain the objective, "Students will be able to describe and exemplify what different plants and animals need to survive."

Next consider the score 2.0. It involves the simpler content the collaborative team has identified. Using the previous example, this score would contain the content regarding terminology and specific facts about plants and animals. The score 4.0 contains the more complex content the collaborative team has identified. In this case, it would be the content regarding the comparison and contrast of plants and animals.

The levels of knowledge collaborative teams identify—the target objective, simpler content, and more complex content—are the meat of each proficiency scale. They constitute scores 2.0, 3.0, and 4.0. The remaining scores in a scale all reference these three levels of knowledge. To illustrate, consider the completed scale in figure 5.6.

Score 4.0	Students will be able to compare and contrast different ways in which plants and animals breathe and find nourishment (for example, comparing and contrasting the fact that plants use their roots and leaves to take in air and food, while animals use their lungs to breathe air and their digestive systems to obtain nourishment).
Score 3.5	In addition to score 3.0 performance, partial success at score 4.0 content
Score 3.0	Students will be able to describe and exemplify what different plants and animals need to survive.
Score 2.5	No major errors or omissions regarding score 2.0 content, and partial success at score 3.0 content
Score 2.0	Students will be able to recall specific terminology such as *plant, animal, survival.* Students will be able to recall details about survival such as: Both plants and animals need food, air, and water to survive. Plants absorb nutrients and air through their roots and leaves. Animals use respiration (lungs) to breathe and digestion to process nutrients.
Score 1.5	Partial success at score 2.0 content, but major errors or omissions regarding score 3.0 content
Score 1.0	With help, partial success at score 2.0 content and score 3.0 content
Score 0.5	With help, partial success at score 2.0 content, but not at score 3.0 content
Score 0.0	Even with help, no success

Copyright Robert J. Marzano. Adapted from Marzano (2009a, pp. 68–69).

Figure 5.6: Scale for survival objective.

In figure 5.6, score values 2.0, 3.0, and 4.0 contain the three levels of content the collaborative team identified. None of the other levels contain new content. For example, a score of 3.5 indicates that a particular student demonstrates competence on score 2.0 and

3.0 content and partial competence in score 4.0 content. A score of 2.5 indicates that a student demonstrates competence on score 2.0 content and partial competence on score 3.0 content. A score of 1.5 indicates that a student demonstrates partial competence in score 2.0 content. The score value of 1.0 does not involve new content; rather, it indicates that without help, a student exhibits little or no competence in any of the content the scale addresses. However, with some help, guidance, and scaffolding, the student demonstrates partial competence in the score 2.0 and 3.0 competence. Score 0.5 indicates that with help, guidance, and scaffolding, the student demonstrates partial competence in the score 2.0 content but not the score 3.0 competence. Finally, a score of 0.0 indicates that even with help, guidance, and scaffolding, the student demonstrates no competence in any of the content articulated in the scale.

In chapter 6, we show how PLCs can use proficiency scales as the driving force in monitoring student progress in an ongoing fashion.

Conclusion

The traditional approach to curriculum in the United States has not served either teachers or students well. This approach has resulted in curriculum overload. A study conducted by the National Governors Association, the Council of Chief State School Officials, and Achieve, Inc. (2008) found that high-performing countries limit the topics students are expected to learn and organize the curriculum around standards that are focused, rigorous, and coherent. In contrast, "state content standards in the U.S. typically cover a large number of topics in each grade level—even first and second grade. U.S. schools therefore end up using curricula that are a 'mile wide and an inch deep'" (p. 24). Another study of American curriculum found:

> There are more state standards at each grade level than any other nation . . . and U.S. teachers cover more topics than teachers in any other country. . . . Our

> teachers work in a context that demands they teach a lot of things, but nothing in-depth. . . . The goal is to teach 35 things briefly, not ten things well. (Schmidt, Houang, & Cogan, 2002, p. 3)

From a vast laundry list of topics, collaborative teams in a PLC must extract a guaranteed and viable curriculum that is relentlessly focused on the most essential learning outcomes for their students. Their success in doing so is vital to the PLC process.

Establishing clarity regarding what students must learn is, however, just one step in the PLC process. Teams must also have a specific process in place for monitoring each student's learning on a timely basis. We turn to that topic in chapter 6.

Ongoing Monitoring of Student Learning

The impact of monitoring on student learning is nearly linear. More monitoring, more achievement. And effective monitoring will focus not just on test scores but on the adult practices that led to the test scores.

—Douglas Reeves

With a guaranteed and viable curriculum like the one described in chapter 5 in place, collaborative teams in PLCs are in a perfect position to monitor student learning in a systematic fashion. Paul Black and Dylan Wiliam (1998a) brought the importance of the ongoing monitoring of student learning to the forefront in the United States. After analyzing findings from over 250 studies on formative assessment, they concluded, "The research reported here shows conclusively that formative assessment does improve learning" (p. 61).

If the potential of formative assessment is to be realized, students, teachers, and administers must undergo a conceptual shift in their approach to assessment. Instead of viewing assessment as an absolute measure of students' proficiency, individual assessments must be considered snapshots taken at a point in time of students' progress toward a specific goal. At the beginning of a unit of instruction, a student might not be close to the desired goal. By the end of the unit, the student might have surpassed the original goal.

If a PLC has developed the proficiency scales for objectives as described in chapter 5, it can easily track and display student progress. To illustrate, consider figure 6.1, which shows scores a student earned on four assessments related to an objective focusing on the topic of transition sentences in essays.

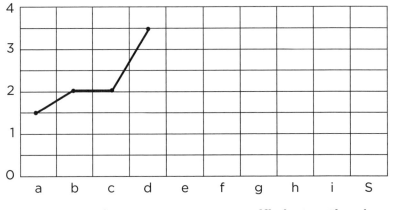

Figure 6.1: Student progress on a specific instructional objective.

The vertical axis in figure 6.1 represents the 0–4.0 scale described in chapter 5. The horizontal axis represents assessments on the objective. Four assessments have been administered over time (assessments *a* through *d*). On the first assessment, the student received a score of 1.5; on the second assessment, she received a score of 2.0, and so on. This type of tracking allows students to see their progress over time. In this case, the student began with a score of 1.5 on the instructional objective and ended with a score of 3.5—a gain of 2.0 points on the scale. This rich, value-added information available to collaborative teams about student progress is at the heart of formative assessment (for a discussion, see Marzano, 2010b).

Assessment in the Current System

To monitor student progress as depicted in figure 6.1, teachers must assess and record assessments in ways that are different from current convention. Before providing our recommendations, it is useful to examine current practices in classroom assessment as a point of contrast.

Whether teachers work independently or in groups, they typically design classroom assessments that cover multiple topics. For example, during a unit in an eighth-grade science class, a teacher might design an assessment that addresses two topics: (1) how climate patterns are affected by the water cycle and (2) how all the levels of the earth's atmosphere are affected by temperature and pressure. For the sake of discussion, let's assume that 35 percent of the points on the test address the first topic and 65 percent of the points address the second topic. Now let's consider two students, both of whom receive a score of 70 percent on the test. While their overall scores are the same, these two students might have a very different understanding of the content, as shown in figure 6.2.

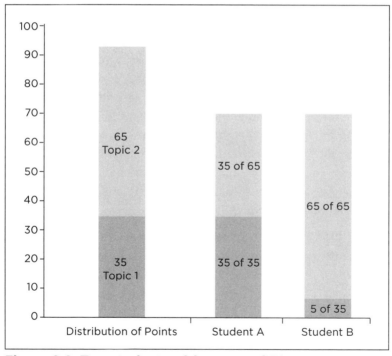

Figure 6.2: Two students with scores of 70 percent.

In figure 6.2, student A scored 70 percent by acquiring 35 of 35 points for the first topic and 35 of 65 points for the second topic. Student B scored 70 percent by acquiring 5 of 35 points for the first topic and 65 of 65 points for the second topic. Clearly, the students have performed very differently on the two topics. Student A seems to know the first topic well, but not the second. Student B has the opposite profile.

As innocent as this might seem, it actually violates a basic tenet of measurement theory: the principle of unidimensionality, which says that every score derived from an assessment should represent one dimension only. Researcher John Hattie (1984, 1985; Hattie, Krakowski, Rogers, & Swaminthan, 1996) has discussed the importance of unidimensionality in the design of assessments:

> A fundamental assumption of test theory is that a score can only have meaning if the set of items measures only one attribute or dimension. If the measurement instrument is composed of items that measure different dimensions, then it is difficult to interpret the total score from a set of items, to make psychological sense when relating variables, or to interpret individual differences. Despite the importance of this assumption to all testing models, there have been few systematic attempts to investigate the assumption and, until recently, little success at providing a defensible procedure to assess the claim of unidimensionality. (Hattie et al., 1996, p. 1)

Designing multidimensional assessments that report single scores only for all dimensions negates any possibility of tracking student progress as depicted in figure 6.1 (page 120). This is so because tracking student progress makes sense only when one dimension is the focus of a set of assessments. Otherwise, a student might actually perform better on a second assessment but receive a lower score.

For example, assume that a mathematics unit addresses two dimensions—one rather easy for a student to understand and the other rather difficult. The first assessment might include both dimensions but focuses mainly on the easier of the two dimensions. Not surprisingly, many students might receive high scores on that initial assessment. Now assume that the second assessment includes both dimensions, but focuses mainly on the more complex dimension. Many of the students who received high scores on the first assessment might receive lower scores on the second assessment, not because they now know less, but simply because the second assessment addressed more difficult content.

Multidimensional assessments, then, create substantial problems in terms of providing students with accurate feedback regarding their progress. Additionally, when assessments include multiple dimensions, as is the current practice, students focus their attention on passing specific assessments as opposed to progressing in their knowledge of the content. In other words, the object of students' attention is scores on tests. A high score—as opposed to increased understanding and skill—is the preeminent goal. As we will see in a subsequent section of this chapter, if an assessment includes multiple dimensions, then students must receive multiple scores.

A New Way to Design and Score Assessments

Using the scales described in chapter 5, teachers can design assessments that are precisely targeted to the levels of content articulated in a scale. To illustrate, consider figure 6.3 (page 124), a scale for the topic of heritable traits.

As described in chapter 5, the objective for the topic of heritable traits occupies the score 3.0 position on the scale. More complex content occupies the score 4.0 position, and simpler content occupies the score 2.0 position. The scale, then, provides a blueprint for designing an assessment. Teachers use the scale to develop items that address the score 2.0 content, items that address the score 3.0 content, and items that address the score 4.0 content. Figure 6.4 (page 125) shows an assessment that includes items for score 2.0, 3.0, and 4.0 content.

Score 4.0	Students will be able to describe how heritable traits and nonheritable traits affect one another.
Score 3.5	In addition to score 3.0 performance, partial success at score 4.0 content
Score 3.0	Students will be able to differentiate heritable traits from nonheritable traits.
Score 2.5	No major errors or omissions regarding score 2.0 content, and partial success at score 3.0 content
Score 2.0	Students will be able to recognize accurate statements about and isolated examples of heritable and nonheritable traits.
Score 1.5	Partial success at score 2.0 content, but major errors or omissions regarding score 3.0 content
Score 1.0	With help, partial success at score 2.0 content and score 3.0 content
Score 0.5	With help, partial success at score 2.0 content, but not at score 3.0 content
Score 0.0	Even with help, no success

Source: Adapted from Marzano (2010b, p. 45).

Figure 6.3: Scale for heritable traits.

Note that figure 6.4 contains three sections—A, B, and C. Section A contains items for the score 2.0 content, section B contains items for the score 3.0 content, and section C contains one item for the score 4.0 content. Of course the teacher would not necessarily have to place all the score 2.0 items together, all the score 3.0 items together, and so on. However, if items at different levels are not organized into sections as depicted in figure 6.4, the teacher must then keep track of the level of difficulty of each item for scoring purposes.

To score an assessment with items at differing levels of difficulty, the teacher does not assign points or rubric scores to individual items as is the current convention. Rather, the teacher scores each item using a coding scheme like the following:

 C = completely correct

 NC = completely incorrect

 P = partial correct

Section A
1. True or false: All diseases are inherited.
2. True or false: If your mom is afraid of roller coasters, you will inherit that fear from her.
3. Examples of inherited traits are _____ and _____.
4. Circle the traits you can develop over time: shoe size, gender, knowledge of history, fear of snakes.
Section B
5. Name three traits you like about yourself. Are these heritable traits or not? Explain your answer.
6. Joey signed up for the summer spelling bee just after Christmas. He did not practice very much because he was playing baseball, and he went to Florida with his parents over spring break. When the bee came, he lost in the first round. Later that night, he told his mother he lost because he is not very smart about words. Do you think this is correct? Why or why not?
7. Simon's mother always asks him to go to the grocery store with her so that he can reach the items on the top shelf. He can reach almost everything she points out. Is this because Simon was born tall, or is it because he has so much practice reaching for items in high places? Has he inherited his ability to reach items on the top shelf? Explain your answer.
Section C
8. Hemophilia is an inherited disease that prevents your blood from clotting. This means that if you ever get a cut or a scrape, you might lose so much blood that it could be life threatening. If you were born with this disease, what kinds of things would you have to avoid? What kinds of things might you be good at instead? What kinds of personality traits might you have that other people might not have? Explain your answer.

Source: Adapted from Marzano (2010b, p. 47).

Figure 6.4: Sample assessment for the topic of heritable traits.

An option that is popular with secondary teachers is to use the following coding scheme:

    C = completely correct

    NC = completely incorrect

    LP = low partial correct

    HP = high partial correct

High partial (HP) means that the student exhibited an understanding of most of the content assessed by the item. Low partial (LP) means that the student exhibited understanding of some, but not the majority of the content assessed by the item.

With each item coded in this fashion, the teacher examines a student's pattern of responses across items to assign an overall scale score for the assessment. For example, assume that a particular student demonstrated the pattern of responses shown in figure 6.5.

Section	Item	Score Value	Item Code
A	1	2.0	C
	2	2.0	C
	3	2.0	C
	4	2.0	C
B	5	3.0	C
	6	3.0	HP
	7	3.0	NC
C	8	4.0	NC

Figure 6.5: Pattern of responses for a specific student.

The student in figure 6.5 answered all score 2.0 items correctly and had some success on the score 3.0 items; however, he did not answer the item correctly for the score 4.0 content. The teacher would assign a scale score of 2.5 for the entire assessment indicating success at the score 2.0 content and partial success at the score 3.0 content.

This approach is quite different from the traditional system of assigning points to each item and then trying to determine how many points each student received on each item. For example, for a test like that in figure 6.4 (page 125), a teacher would typically assign points to the types of items using a scheme like the following: each item in section A receives 2 points, each item in section B receives 5 points, and the single item in section B receives 10 points. Using this scheme, it would probably be fairly easy to score the items in section A; each item would receive 0 points, 1 point, or 2 points. However, scoring the items in section B would be more problematic. While it would be easy to assign a score of 0 points if the answer is completely incorrect or a score of 5 points if the answer is completely correct, it would be difficult to discern whether an answer should receive 2, 3, or 4 points for partial correctness. The problem is even more severe for item 8 in section C. Again, it would be easy to assign a score of 10 for a completely correct answer and a score of 0 for a completely incorrect answer, but how would a teacher reliably discern how to assign a score of 2, 3, 4, 5, 6, 7, 8, or 9 for partially correct answers?

The system we have depicted in figure 6.5 that codes items as completely correct, completely incorrect, low partial, and high partial correctness has been shown to be much easier for teachers to use and produces much higher reliability for teacher-designed tests (for a discussion see Marzano, 2002).

Of course, the student's responses charted in figure 6.5 depict a fairly straightforward pattern. Often teachers ask what happens if a student's scores depict aberrant patterns, such as doing well on score 3.0 content but not on score 2.0 content. The solutions to such issues are discussed in some depth in Marzano (2006). Briefly, though, an aberrant pattern can occur for a number of reasons, including the following:

- The items written for a particular score value were flawed in some way.

- Students put effort into answering some items but not others.

- The teacher's evaluation of student responses was inaccurate.

A teacher can do many things to reconcile the issue of aberrant patterns of responses, including the following:

- Ignore items that appear to be aberrant.

- Meet with individual students who display such patterns, and ask them to explain the reasoning behind their answers.

- Return the test to students who display aberrant patterns, and ask them to redo specific items.

- Reclassify items at a higher or lower score value based on the responses of the entire class.

Tests With Multiple Dimensions

Given the importance of unidimensionality to the theory base for effective testing, we recommend that, if at all possible, assessments should be designed to measure one dimension. An assessment could, however, include more than one dimension, provided scores are computed and reported for *each dimension* in the assessment. For example, assume that a mathematics test measures both ability to perform basic computations and ability to graph linear equations from a set of ordered pairs. These are two different dimensions. A student might be poor at basic computations but quite knowledgeable about graphing linear equations from a set of ordered pairs (or vice versa). As we saw in figure 6.2 (page 121), assigning a single score to this assessment might mask important information about students' strengths and weaknesses. Two students could receive the same overall single score yet have opposite profiles for the two underlying dimensions in the test.

The procedure for designing a multidimensional test would be tantamount to designing two separate assessments and then combining them. Teams would develop items for score 2.0, 3.0, and 4.0 content for both dimensions. Teachers would then score a set of items for each dimension as depicted in figure 6.5 (page 126). Of course the teacher scoring the assessment would have to keep in mind which items were associated with which dimensions. Finally, the teacher would compute a scale score for each dimension and report back to each student. There would not be an overall score to report for the test.

To use another example, consider a set of objectives for the topic of writing effective expository essays. As described in chapter 5, a PLC might identify the following five objectives under this topic:

1. Students will include in their expository essays a clear thesis statement accompanied by support and qualifiers that limit the scope of their claims.

2. Students will include in their expository essays clear transitions between paragraphs and sections.

3. Students will include in their expository essays clear reference regarding subject/verb agreement and clear reference for pronouns.

4. Students will include in their expository essays word choices that are not redundant but communicate a clear message.

5. Students will include in their expository essays beginning-of-sentence capitalization and end-of-sentence punctuation that is appropriate to the essay.

While a teacher might single out each of these objectives for a lesson or set of lessons, he or she could also assign an expository essay to students and score it based on each of the five objectives. Since teams developed proficiency scales for each of the five objectives, the teacher could assign five scores per essay—one for each of the objectives. This would provide students with a panoramic view of their profile across the five skills that constitute the process (the macroprocedure) of writing expository essays.

New Types of Assessments

In addition to a different way of designing and scoring assessments, the scales in chapter 5 also allow for effective use of assessments other than the traditional pencil-and-paper test. Following are three alternate forms of assessments made possible by proficiency scales.

Probing Discussions

Probing discussions are a unique form of assessment that are well suited to proficiency scales. Simply stated, during a probing discussion a teacher meets with a student and asks him or her to explain specific information or demonstrate a specific skill or process while the teacher asks questions. As explained by Marzano (2010b):

> The teacher meets one-on-one with a particular student and asks him or her to explain or demonstrate something. For example, during a unit on relationships found in nature, a middle school science teacher might sit next to a student and ask her to explain the similarities and differences between mutualism, symbiosis, and commensalism. As the student explains these concepts, the teacher would ask probing questions that help to clarify what she knows and does not know. The scale that had been designed for this content would guide the teacher as to the types of questions he should ask to determine the scale score that most accurately represents the student's status at that point in time. (p. 71)

Unobtrusive Assessments

Unobtrusive assessments are most easily applied to procedural knowledge, particularly that from the psychomotor domain, because such knowledge is observable. Marzano (2010b) describes unobtrusive assessments in the following way:

> [In an unobtrusive assessment] a teacher might "catch" a student performing a skill, strategy, or process in a natural setting. For example, consider the physical skill of hitting a baseball. A physical education teacher might observe a student hitting a softball during recess and record this observation as a formative score. Similarly,

an art teacher might observe a student executing a particular type of brushstroke in class and record this observation as a formative score. (p. 74)

Student-Generated Assessments

Student-generated assessments are probably the most powerful and revolutionary form of assessments made available by performance scales. Here students approach the teacher and propose what they will do to demonstrate they have achieved a particular status on a proficiency scale. Marzano (2010b) provides the following examples from language arts, mathematics, science, and social studies:

Language arts: To demonstrate score 3.0 competence for a learning goal [the instructional objective] regarding spelling, an elementary student proposes he take a short verbal test with the teacher after school.

Mathematics: To demonstrate score 3.0 competence in graphing linear equations, a student proposes she solve and graph the equations in the practice section of the textbook.

Science: A student who wants to demonstrate score 3.0 competence in physical science for a learning goal [the instructional objective] involving combustibility proposes he bring in a short video clip of the Hindenburg disaster and explain step-by-step what caused the explosion.

Social Studies: To demonstrate score 3.0 competence in U.S. history for a learning goal [the instructional objective] regarding the civil rights movement, a student proposes she create a timeline that includes the major relevant events of that time. Furthermore, she thinks she can demonstrate score 4.0 competence if she sits down with the teacher after creating the timeline to discuss how one event affected another and how this cause-and-effect chain created the momentum for a movement. (pp. 75–76)

SMART Goals Reconsidered

Scales and their related assessments put SMART goals in a new perspective. DuFour, DuFour, Eaker, and Many (2010) provide the following examples of SMART goals, which we introduced in chapter 1:

Last year, 86 percent of the grades assigned to our students were passing grades.

This year, we will increase the percentage of passing grades to at least 93 percent.

Last year, 76 percent of our students met the proficiency standard on the state math test.

This year, we will increase the percentage of students meeting the proficiency standard on the state math test to 80 percent or higher. (pp. 158–159)

SMART goals at this level are still quite useful, even when teams have developed proficiency scales. Those scales, however, also allow for identifying more specific SMART goals around performance on specific proficiency scales. For example, after designing a scale and accompanying assessments for a particular topic in algebra I, a collaborative team might set the following SMART goal:

By the end of the quarter, 100 percent of students in the class will have gained at least two points on the proficiency scale.

By the end of the quarter, 80 percent of students will be at score value 3.0 or above.

Common Assessments Reconsidered

Larry Ainsworth and Donald Viegut (2006) have chronicled the development of common assessments and illustrated the important role these assessments play in monitoring student progress. We cannot overstate the importance of common assessments to the PLC process. As Rick and his colleagues wrote:

> Instead of individual teachers developing and administering a summative test at the end of a unit, a collaborative team of teachers responsible for the same course or grade level creates a common *formative* assessment before teaching a unit. Members of the team agree on the standard students must achieve to be deemed proficient and establish when they will give the assessment. (DuFour et al., 2008, p. 208)

Rick and his colleagues go on to explain that immediately after the assessment is administered, members of the team analyze the results to determine appropriate actions they can take in class and to identify students who require additional support through the school's system of intervention. Thus, the common assessment provides focused data used by team members to optimize their instructional effectiveness.

Proficiency scales can make the process of designing and interpreting common assessments highly efficient. Once scales are constructed, assessments are fairly easy to design: teachers simply create assessment items for the score 2.0, 3.0, and 4.0 content. Scales also allow teachers to design their unique individual assessments but still maintain a common interpretation of a standard to score on those assessments. For example, two teachers responsible for an algebra I course might design two tests that are quite different in format; however, scores for students in the two classes will be directly comparable when proficiency scales are used, provided the team has practiced applying the proficiency scale score until they have established inter-rater reliability. A score of 2.5 means that a student has demonstrated complete knowledge of the score 2.0 content and partial understanding of the score 3.0 content, regardless of which test was given and which teacher scored the test. Finally, scales allow teachers to use other types of assessments, such as probing discussions, unobtrusive assessment, and student-generated assessments.

Translating Scale Scores to Traditional Grades

Proficiency scales represent a dramatic shift in the metric used to evaluate students. Instead of students receiving scores from 0 to 100 on tests, students receive scale scores that range from 0 to 4.0. As demonstrated in figure 6.2 on page 121, the 100-point scale does not provide very accurate or useful information about student performance, particularly when assessments are multidimensional in nature. However, most grading policies currently in use, particularly at the middle school and high school levels, are based on the 100-point scale. Consequently, teachers might have to translate the proficiency scale scores into a 100-point metric. There are many schemes for doing this (for a discussion see Marzano, 2010b). A popular one used by secondary teachers appears in figure 6.6.

Scale Score	Translation to 100-Point Scale
4.0	100
3.5	95
3.0	90
2.5	80
2.0	70
1.5	65
1.0	50
0.5	25
0.0	0

Figure 6.6: Conversion scheme for translating proficiency scale into 100-point scale.

While there are certainly other translation schemes teachers could use, the scale in figure 6.6 seems to have an intuitive appeal to teachers and preserves the integrity of the scale, at least to some extent. Understand, however, that any translation from one scale to another usually introduces error in measurement and interpretation. We offer the scheme in figure 6.6 as a tool that allows teachers to use proficiency scales even though their school or district requires the use of the conventional 100-point scale. Of course, this is not an optimal situation.

A New Report Card

While the creation of proficiency scales does not require a new type of report card, it can be used as a catalyst for designing new report cards. In fact, new report cards become a very logical alternative when a district or school has articulated proficiency scales for all the content in a course or at a grade level. Report cards like the one in figure 6.7 on pages 136–138 are a viable alternative to traditional report cards when proficiency scales are in place.

Figure 6.7 shows a sample report card for fourth grade, but the same format can be easily used in grades K–12. For the purposes of this discussion, we will assume that the school is departmentalized for each subject, so different teachers are responsible for different subject areas. For this grading period, five subject areas have been addressed: language arts, mathematics, science, social studies, and art. The student represented in figure 6.7 has received a score of 2.5 for word recognition and vocabulary, 1.5 for main idea, and so on within the subject of language arts.

It is important to recognize that each bar graph in figure 6.7 has a dark base and a light top. The darkened part at the base of each bar represents the student's scale score at the beginning of the grading period. For example, while the student in figure 6.7 received a final score of 2.5 for the topic of word recognition and vocabulary, he began the grading period with a score of 1.0. In other words, the grey part at the top of each bar graph reports the knowledge gain for a student on each topic. The student in figure 6.7 gained 1.5 proficiency-scale points for the topic of word recognition and vocabulary, 1.0 proficiency-scale points for reading for main idea, and so on.

Name:	John Mark													
Address:	123 Some Street													
City:	Anytown, CO 80000													
Grade Level:	4													
Homeroom:	Ms. Smith													

Language Arts	2.46	C		Participation	3.40	A			
Mathematics	2.50	B		Work Completion	2.90	B			
Science	2.20	C		Behavior	3.40	A			
Social Studies	3.10	A		Working in Groups	2.70	B			
Art	3.00	A							

Language Arts		
Reading:		
Word Recognition and Vocabulary	2.5	
Reading for Main Idea	1.5	
Literary Analysis	2.0	
Writing:		
Language Conventions	3.5	
Organization and Focus	2.5	
Research and Technology	1.0	
Evaluation and Revision	2.5	
Writing Applications	3.0	
Listening and Speaking:		
Comprehension	3.0	
Organization and Delivery	3.0	
Analysis and Evaluation of Oral Media	2.5	
Speaking Applications	2.5	
Life Skills:		
Participation	4.0	
Work Completion	3.5	
Behavior	3.5	
Working in Groups	3.0	
Average for Language Arts	2.46	

Mathematics		
Number Systems	3.5	
Estimation	3.0	
Addition/Subtraction	2.5	
Multiplication/Division	2.5	
Ratio/Proportion/Percent	1.0	
Life Skills:		
Participation	4.0	
Work Completion	2.0	
Behavior	3.5	
Working in Groups	2.0	
Average for Mathematics	2.50	
Science		
Matter and Energy	2.0	
Forces of Nature	2.5	
Diversity of Life	1.5	
Human Identity	3.5	
Interdependence of Life	1.5	
Life Skills:		
Participation	3.0	
Work Completion	1.5	
Behavior	2.5	
Working in Groups	1.0	
Average for Science	2.20	
Social Studies		
The Influence of Culture	3.5	
Current Events	3.0	
Personal Responsibility	4.0	
Government Representation	3.5	
Human and Civil Rights	1.5	
Life Skills:		
Participation	3.5	
Work Completion	3.5	

Figure 6.7: Sample report card for fourth grade.

Continued on next page →

Behavior	3.5										
Working in Groups	4.0										
Average for Social Studies	3.10										
Art											
Purposes of Art	3.5										
Art Skills	3.0										
Art and Culture	2.5										
Life Skills:											
Participation	2.5										
Work Completion	4.0										
Behavior	4.0										
Working in Groups	3.5										
Average for Art	3.00										

Copyright 2007 Marzano & Associates. All rights reserved.

Also note that in each subject area reported in figure 6.7, the student has received proficiency-scale scores for the life-skill topics of participation, work completion, behavior, and working in groups. Collaborative teams can develop proficiency scales for these skills just as they can for academic objectives (for a discussion, see Marzano & Haystead, 2008). While proficiency scale scores for these life-skill topics are reported for each subject, those scores are not counted when computing the letter grade for the subject areas.

Finally, note that the report card includes traditional letter grades for each subject area. These are calculated by directly translating proficiency scales scores into traditional grades using a conversion scheme like the one in figure 6.8.

As shown in figure 6.8, if a student receives an average score across topics of 3.51 to 4.00, the student would receive an A. An average score of 3.00 to 3.50 translates to a grade of A–, and so on. The scheme in figure 6.8 is not the only valid translation scheme, but it does represent the general pattern used by a number of schools that have adopted the proficiency scale system.

Average Scale Score	Traditional Grade	Average Scale Score	Traditional Grade
3.51–4.00	A	2.17–2.33	C
3.00–3.50	A–	2.00–2.16	C–
2.84–2.99	B+	1.84–1.99	D+
2.6–2.83	B	1.67–1.83	D
2.50–2.66	B–	1.50–1.66	D–
2.34–2.49	C+	.00–1.49	F

Source: Adapted from Marzano (2010b, p. 106)

Figure 6.8: Conversion scheme for translating proficiency scale into traditional grades.

Ongoing monitoring of student learning is one of the most powerful tools available to PLC collaborative teams for enhancing student achievement. This monitoring requires *collective* analysis of results and their implications for changes in teacher practice (Hattie, 2009; Timperley & Alton-Lee, 2008). The proficiency scales described in chapter 5 and the assessment techniques described in this chapter allow for increased precision when providing feedback to students and offer a powerful tool to support the collective inquiry of collaborative teams.

Conclusion

The longstanding practice in American education has been for individual teachers to use assessment to provide a student with the opportunity to demonstrate his or her learning at the appointed time. The standard pattern has been, "Teach, test, hope for the best, assign a grade, and move on to the next unit." Assessment has been used as a tool for sorting students into "our A students, our B students," and so on.

The creation of team-based common assessments is an absolutely vital step in the PLC journey. If, however, teams continue to use common assessments merely to assign grades before moving to the next unit, little progress will be made. The assessment process in a PLC is not used simply to *prove* what a student has learned, but to *improve* that learning. Until members of collaborative teams are using the results from common assessments to identify and respond to the specific learning needs of each student and to analyze and improve their individual and collective professional practice, that school is most assuredly *not* a PLC.

CHAPTER 7

Ensuring Effective Instruction

> What distinguishes professional learning communities
> from support groups where teachers mainly share
> ideas and offer encouragement is their critical stance
> and commitment to inquiry. . . . Teachers ask probing
> questions, invite colleagues to observe and review
> their teaching and their students' learning, and hold
> out ideas for discussion and debate.
>
> —Jonathon Saphier

Effective classroom assessment as described in chapter 6 is a powerful tool for enhancing student achievement. With clear objectives embedded in scales that form a guaranteed and viable curriculum, and with specific details regarding what constitutes the different levels of performance for an objective, students will have the benefit of knowing what they are expected to learn and what they must do to demonstrate their learning. When effective instruction is added to this mix, the effect on student achievement increases even more. In this chapter, we consider how to design and deliver lessons that maximize the probability that all students will acquire the intended knowledge and skills.

Effective instruction is explicit in the first big idea of a PLC: ensuring that all students learn at high levels. It follows then that one of the major responsibilities of teams in a PLC is the planning and delivery of lessons that lead to high levels of learning.

Any chapter on effective instruction must, however, begin with a caveat. No single instructional strategy is guaranteed to result in high levels of student learning. Even strategies that have a solid research base supporting their effectiveness are likely to be found ineffective by a substantial number of other studies assessing the impact of those same strategies. The lesson here is simple:

> Educators must always look to whether a particular strategy is producing the desired results as opposed to simply assuming that if a strategy is being used, positive results will ensue. If a strategy doesn't appear to be working well, educators must adapt the strategy as needed or use other strategies. This is yet another reason why teachers shouldn't be required to use specific strategies. Since none are guaranteed to work, teachers must have the freedom and flexibility to adapt or try something different when student learning isn't forthcoming. (Marzano, 2009b, p. 35)

Put another way, "The ultimate criterion for successful teaching should be student knowledge gain" (Marzano, 2009b, p. 37). Instruction is a means to an end—student learning—and thus the ultimate test of effective instruction is actual evidence that students have learned. The story of the doctor who proclaimed, "The operation was a success, but the patient died" would hold no credence in a PLC. The most important criterion in assessing the success of a lesson is whether or not students have learned.

Lesson Study

The idea that teachers should work collaboratively in thinking through effective lessons is certainly not new. The collective development of highly crafted lessons is a fundamental aspect of *kounaikenshuu*, a comprehensive set of activities that form the crux of school improvement in Japan. Stigler and Hiebert (1999) wrote:

> One of the most common components of *kounaikenshuu* is lesson study (*jugyou kenkyuu*). In lesson study, groups of teachers meet regularly over long periods of time (ranging from several months to a year) to work on the design, implementation, testing, and improvement of one or several "research designs" (*kenkyuu jugyou*). By all indicators, lesson study is extremely

popular and highly valued by Japanese teachers, espe-
cially at the elementary level. It is the linchpin of the
improvement process. (pp. 110–111)

Since the introduction of the concept of lesson study to U. S. educators by Stigler and Hiebert, a number of adaptations have been
developed (see, for example, Jalongo, Rieg, & Helterbran, 2007).
None of the current U.S. versions of lesson study, however, have
been specifically adapted for use within a PLC as described in this
book. The collaborative teams within PLCs are perfect vehicles for
developing and vetting effective lessons, and those teams should
engage in their own form of *jugyou kenkyuu*, or lesson study, at a
very detailed level. For each objective and each scale, specific lessons can be designed and vetted during the course of the school
year. Just as a national archive of effective lessons is continually
growing in Japan, so too can a school-based (or district-based)
archive of effective lessons be developed in PLC schools.

Lesson Study Within a PLC

In chapter 5, we saw that academic content can be classified into
three broad categories: (1) information, (2) mental procedures, and
(3) psychomotor procedures. We also saw that to develop a guaranteed and viable curriculum, rubrics or scales should be designed
to include three levels of content knowledge. Each level of knowledge requires a different type of instruction. Consequently, when
engaged in lesson study, collaborative teams should think in terms
of three different types of lessons for each scale they have created.
We consider lesson study for informational knowledge first.

Lesson Study for Information

Once again, information can be classified into two broad categories: organizing ideas and details. When writing scales, collaborative teams commonly include organizing ideas (generalizations and principles) as the score 3.0 content, and details (time

sequences, facts, and vocabulary terms) as the score 2.0 content. To illustrate, consider figure 7.1.

Score	Content
4.0	Students predict and defend possible changes in the Bill of Rights in the 21st century.
3.5	In addition to score 3.0 performance, partial success at score 4.0 content
3.0	Students demonstrate an understanding of the influence of political rights on individuals and society in general with specific focus on the Bill of Rights within the U.S. Constitution.
2.5	No major errors or omissions regarding score 2.0 content, and partial success at score 3.0 content
2.0	Students recall or recognize important details about the U.S. Constitution and the Bill of Rights such as: • Important terms and phrases including *right to petition, freedom of press, U.S. Constitution, Bill of Rights* • Important facts including the general history of the Bill of Rights and the more well-known elements of the Bill of Rights, like the First Amendment
1.5	Partial success at score 2.0 content, but major errors or omissions regarding score 3.0 content
1.0	With help, partial success at score 2.0 content and score 3.0 content
0.5	With help, partial success at score 2.0 content, but not at score 3.0 content
0.0	Even with help, no success

Figure 7.1: A scale for information.

In figure 7.1, score 3.0 involves the generalization that the Bill of Rights in the U.S. Constitution has had an influence on the lives of individuals as well as society as a whole. Score 2.0 involves facts and vocabulary terms that are considered important to a full understanding of that generalization. Score 4.0 content involves extrapolating from the generalization of the instructional objective to possible future events during the 21st century.

Planning for Score 2.0 Informational Content

Score 2.0 content typically involves details when the focus of a scale is informational content. Details provide the foundation for organizing ideas like generalizations and principles. For example, in figure 7.1. the details include important terms and phrases like *right to petition, freedom of press, U.S. Constitution,* and *Bill of Rights.* Certainly each of these elements is a very complex topic in its own right; however, when complex topics are listed as score 2.0 content, the expectation is that students simply have a surface-level understanding of them as opposed to a more complete grasp of their meaning. For example, a more robust understanding of the right to petition would include the information in figure 7.2.

The right to petition is expressly set out in the First Amendment:

"Congress shall make no law . . . abridging . . . the right of the people . . . to petition the Government for a redress of griev-ances."
—from the First Amendment

The petition clause concludes the First Amendment's enumera-tion of expressive rights and, in many ways, supports them all. *Petition* is the right to ask government at any level to right a wrong or correct a problem.

The right to petition allows citizens to focus government atten-tion on unresolved ills; provides information to elected leaders about unpopular policies; exposes misconduct, waste, corrup-tion, and incompetence; and vents popular frustrations without endangering the public order.

Petitioning was a form of public dialogue as far back as colo-nial days. Two hundred years later, petitioning has become an instrument of mass politics, designed to make a point, not a plea. As with the divisive issue of slavery, petitioning is now seen as a means of uniting popular groups and overwhelming political opponents.

Figure 7.2: Information regarding the Bill of Rights.

Continued on next page →

Petitioning has come to signify any nonviolent, legal means of encouraging or disapproving government action, whether directed to the judicial, executive, or legislative branch. Lobbying, letter writing, email campaigns, testifying before tribunals, filing lawsuits, supporting referenda, collecting signatures for ballot initiatives, peaceful protests and picketing: all public articulation of issues, complaints, and interests designed to spur government action qualify under the petition clause, even if the activities partake of other First Amendment freedoms.

Yet despite its social benefits, the First Amendment right of petition has not been developed as a doctrine or championed as a cause. Few scholars or courts have fully appreciated the importance of the right to petition and its more contemporary applications.

Perhaps the right of petition has escaped their attention precisely *because* it continues to work so well. The petition clause is the tacit assumption in constitutional analysis, the primordial right from which other expressive freedoms arise. Why speak, why publish, why assemble against the government at all if such complaints will only be silenced?

As Justice John Paul Stevens stressed in his dissent in *Minnesota Board for Community Colleges*, "The First Amendment was intended to secure something more than an exercise in futility." The petition clause ensures that our leaders hear, even if they don't listen to, the electorate. Though public officials may be indifferent, contrary, or silent participants in democratic discourse, at least the First Amendment commands their audience.

Source: Adapted from Newton and Collins (2008).

When a complex topic like the right to petition is listed as score 2.0 content, the expectation is that students understand only superficial but important information. For example, the expectation might be that students know the following about the right to petition:

- The right to petition is specifically stated in the First Amendment.

- The right to petition states that the people can ask the government to correct perceived problems.

The same is true regarding the facts listed in the scale in figure 7.1 (page 144). The expectation is that students understand some facts about the Bill of Rights, such as the following:

- The Bill of Rights spells out the rights of individual citizens.

- The Bill of Rights was added to the U.S. Constitution to keep the government from exerting too much control over the lives of the citizens.

Again, there is no expectation that these facts represent a comprehensive or even a general understanding of the topic. Rather, these facts exist for students as isolated pieces of information that provide a basis for learning the more complex score 3.0 generalization about the Bill of Rights.

Teaching score 2.0 informational content is a fairly straightforward process. When collaborative teams plan a lesson to introduce score 2.0 content, they should consider doing the following:

- Organizing students into small groups

- Helping students preview the content

- Chunking the content into small "digestible bites"

- Scaffolding the chunks

- Allowing students to process each chunk

- Asking elaborative questions

- Having students represent the content in linguistic and/or nonlinguistic ways

- Having students reflect on their own learning

It is important to note that teachers would have flexibility to divert from the activities planned by cooperative teams. The lesson plans cooperative teams develop should never be thought of as scripts that all teachers must follow. Rather, they represent blueprints that teachers might divert from when it is evident that those strategies are not working.

The specifics of this instructional sequence are described in detail in Marzano (2007) and Marzano and Brown (2009). Briefly though, the first step in the process is to organize students into small groups (interaction groups) of two or three students. These groups might be established in an ad hoc fashion at the beginning of a class period, or they might be established for an entire unit of instruction. During the next unit, students are assigned to a new group to ensure that students have different partners throughout the school year.

Before presenting new content, the teacher would help students preview the content. There are many ways this can be done:

- Asking students what they already know about the content

- Providing students with a brief overview of the content

- Providing students with a graphic organizer depicting the new content

- Providing students with a partially filled-in outline of the new content

The specific strategy to use could be the subject of discussion by collaborative teams.

The next two elements—chunking and scaffolding—are related. *Chunking* refers to organizing the content into small digestible bites. Each chunk should be small and concise enough so as not to tax students' short-term memories. The size of each chunk is determined by how much students already know about the content. The more students know about the content, the larger the chunk.

Chunking is influenced by the medium that is used to introduce the content. For example, if a collaborative team planned to use a video clip to introduce score 2.0 content about the Bill of Rights, members would determine the points during which the video would be stopped and students would be asked to process the content. If using a lecture to introduce information about the

Bill of Rights, team members would identify appropriate places to pause in the lecture.

Scaffolding is closely related to chunking. *Scaffolding* involves organizing the introduction of the knowledge in such a way that one chunk is linked to the next. With informational content, particularly when it involves details, the linkages between chunks might not be very strong. For example, a teacher does not have to address the general intent of the right to petition before addressing information about its history. However, when addressing mental procedures and psychomotor procedures, we will see that some chunks of content are prerequisites for other chunks. Collaborative teams should carefully think through how to sequence different chunks to optimize student learning. This might mean that they alter the manner in which content is presented in textbooks, DVDs, articles, and the like. For example, a collaborative team might determine that students should read the last few pages in the chapter of a text first since it presents information that will provide a firm foundation for other information that will be presented during an introductory lesson.

Allowing students to process the information in each chunk can take many forms. It might be as simple as having students verbally summarize the information in a chunk in their interactive groups. Responsibility for generating a summary might rotate from member to member after each chunk. Alternatively, after the teacher presents a chunk, he or she might provide interaction groups with a question they are to answer or ask them to generate a question of their own. Collaborative teams would plan various activities for processing the content of each chunk and could use different interaction activities for each chunk.

Once students have processed the chunks of content, teachers can ask elaborative questions that help students think beyond what was presented. Typically, these questions are inferential. For example, after processing four chunks of information about the topic of the Bill of Rights, teachers might ask students questions such as the following: Why do you think the founders of our country did not initially include the Bill of Rights when they first wrote the Constitution?

The penultimate step in the instructional sequence calls upon students to represent the content they have processed in linguistic and/or nonlinguistic ways. This step requires students to synthesize what they have learned. Again, there are many ways this can be done. On the linguistic side, students might be asked to:

- Write a brief summary of what they have learned

- Write an outline of what they have learned

- Write individual notes regarding the content they have learned

On the nonlinguistic side, students might be asked to:

- Create a graphic organizer for the content they have learned

- Draw a sketch or pictograph for the content they have learned

- Physically act out what they have learned

- Create a poster representing what they have learned

- Draw a political cartoon representing what they have learned

Again, during lesson design, collaborative teams plan the types of linguistic and nonlinguistic representations teachers might use during the introduction of score 2.0 content. For example, for the introductory lesson on the Bill of Rights, a team might recommend the use of summaries generated by each student group. After each student team shares its summaries, the whole class might generate a graphic representation with the teacher's guidance on a large piece of chart paper, which is then displayed in class.

The last step in the recommended sequence for introducing score 2.0 informational content is to ask students to briefly reflect on their own learning. A common technique is for students to respond to a prompt by the teacher like the following:

- What is the most significant thing you learned in this lesson?

- What are you interested in learning more about?

- What are you still wondering about?

Students might record their responses to prompts like these in academic notebooks or journals that they keep and occasionally hand in to the teacher for review. Another option is to ask students to record their responses on a note card that is given to the teacher as they exit the class.

A well-designed introductory lesson addressing all these elements provides teachers with a blueprint for effective instruction. Such lessons not only detail the instructional activities that might occur and the recommended sequence of those activities, but they also provide specific information about the resources necessary to execute the lesson and where teachers might obtain those resources.

Planning for Score 3.0 Informational Content

With a foundation of important details, students can more powerfully examine generalizations and principles. Again, consider the generalization stated in the score 3.0 content in figure 7.1 (page 144): the Bill of Rights in the U.S. Constitution has had an influence on the lives of individuals as well as society as a whole. Understanding this generalization means that students can generate examples of it independently. Indeed, *it is the ability to generate examples that defines an understanding of a generalization or a principle.* To illustrate, assume that a student could recite the generalization, but when asked to provide an example, he could not. This would indicate mere rote memorization of a sentence.

Lessons that are designed to help students develop the ability to generate examples begin with the teacher providing clear examples and articulating why they are, in fact, examples. Therefore, collaborative teams engaged in lesson design for these types of lessons would identify specific examples that teachers might present and explain to students.

Concept attainment is a powerful instructional strategy to assist students in developing examples. Popularized by Joyce and Weil (1986) but based on the work of Bruner (1973), the strategy asks students to contrast examples and nonexamples of the construct they are examining. Marzano (2007) adapts an example provided by Joyce and Weil involving an eighth-grade social studies teacher whose class has been examining the characteristics of the fourteen largest cities in the United States. The teacher has provided students with data on the size, ethnicity of population, types of industries, location, and proximity to natural resources:

> This information has been organized into charts for each city, which are displayed around the room for all students to see. With this setting as a backdrop, the teacher explains to the class that she is going to present information a bit differently. She tells students that some of the cities represent certain concepts, whereas others do not. She explains that she will provide one concept at a time. With each concept, she will provide examples and nonexamples. She starts by saying, "Houston, Texas, is an example of the concept I'm thinking of. It's a 'yes.'" The students immediately look at the chart for Houston to examine its characteristics. The teacher then points to the chart for Baltimore, Maryland, and says that it is a "no." She also points to the chart for San Jose, California, and says it is a "yes."
>
> Next, the teacher asks if anyone can guess what she is thinking about. A few students raise their hands. The teacher acknowledges their progress but tells them to keep their guesses private for a while. She then asks them to test their guesses using the next examples and nonexamples, explaining that Seattle, Washington, and Miami, Florida, are "yeses," but Detroit, Michigan, is a "no." She continues until all students think they have identified the concept, and only then does the teacher ask students to share their ideas regarding the characteristics that link all the "yes" cities. This

sharing is done in groups of three. Students come to
a common understanding that the concept is "rapidly growing cities that have relatively mild climates."
Students are then asked to state this new concept in
their own words. The process is repeated two more
times for two additional concepts about large cities in
the United States. (pp. 47–48)

A team using this strategy for the lesson on the Bill of Rights
would provide students with some clear examples of how the Bill
of Rights has influenced the lives of individuals and society as a
whole. Teachers would then create activities that require students
to generate and defend their own examples. If students cannot correctly generate or defend their own examples, the teacher should
provide more examples. This relates directly to one of the critical
questions embedded within the first big idea of a PLC: how will
we respond when students do not learn? If students cannot perform the activities designed for score 3.0 content, then teachers
must respond by clarifying examples or providing new examples.
It might also be the case that teachers must go back to some of
the foundational score 2.0 content that students might not have
learned at an adequate level.

To design lessons of this nature that include a great many examples and nonexamples would require considerable time on the part
of individual teachers if they approach the task in isolation and
attempt to prepare the lesson on their own. By working in collaborative teams to develop such lessons, teachers greatly decrease
preparation time. Furthermore, after they have developed the initial lesson, the team can work to enhance the lesson in subsequent
years.

Planning for Score 4.0 Informational Content

Score 4.0 content typically requires students to make inferences
and applications that go beyond what was addressed in class.
For score 4.0 content, the job of collaborative teams is to design
tasks that require inferences about and applications of knowledge.

Marzano and Kendall (2007, 2008) have identified a number of tasks that serve this purpose. They are described in figure 7.3.

Comparison tasks: These tasks require students to identify and explain how information that has been addressed in class is similar to and different from information that has not been presented in class. For example, a collaborative team might design a task that asks students to compare the Bill of Rights to some other document that has nothing to do with the Constitution.

Classification tasks: These tasks require students to organize content addressed in class into categories that have not been addressed in class. For example, a collaborative team might design a task that asks student to organize the amendments into two or more categories and defend why specific amendments are placed into specific categories.

Error analysis tasks: These tasks require students to identify logical or factual errors others have applied to information presented in class. For example, a collaborative team might design a task that asks students to find a misapplication of a particular amendment and explain why it is a misapplication of the amendment.

Inductive inference tasks: These tasks require students to generate and defend a new generalization regarding content addressed in class. For example, a collaborative team might design a task that requires students to create a generalization about the Bill of Rights that was not directly addressed in class and defend how the information that was addressed in class supports this generalization.

Deductive inference tasks: These tasks require students to make predictions and then defend their predictions based on rules or principles regarding the content addressed in class. For example, a collaborative team might design a task that requires students to make a prediction regarding changes that might occur to the Bill of Rights and then defend their predictions using principles or rules that have been established about the Bill of Rights.

Figure 7.3: Tasks that require inferences and applications.

Teachers might present students with a number of tasks like those in figure 7.3. Student completion of any of these tasks could be used to demonstrate score 4.0 status. Alternatively, a collaborative team might identify a specific type of task that must be used to demonstrate score 4.0 status. This is the case in figure 7.1 on page 144. Score 4.0 specifies that students must complete a deductive inference task regarding predictions about future changes in the Bill of Rights.

Summary of Lesson Study for Information

To engage in lesson study for information, collaborative teams would design introductory lessons for score 2.0 content that involve instructional activities for organizing students into interaction groups, previewing the content, chunking the content into small bites, scaffolding the chunks, allowing students to process each chunk, asking elaborative questions, asking students to represent the content in linguistic and/or nonlinguistic forms, and asking students to reflect on their learning. While engaged in lesson design for score 3.0 content, collaborative teams would identify clear examples and nonexamples, design tasks that require students to recognize examples and nonexamples, and require students to generate and defend examples and nonexamples. Finally, while engaged in lesson design for score 4.0 content, collaborative teams would design tasks that require students to make inferences about and applications of score 3.0 content. Tasks typically used to this end involve comparison, classification, error analysis, inductive inferences, and deductive inferences.

Lesson Study for Mental Procedures

Mental procedures address knowledge of how to do something, such as being able to edit a composition for overall logic, solving a specific type of problem in mathematics, or reading for the purpose of synthesizing a long passage into a succinct summary. Mental procedures can be organized into two broad categories: processes and skills. As described in chapter 5, processes are complex procedures that usually include multiple interacting skills. Instructional objectives are usually written at the skill level. Consider the scale in figure 7.4 (page 156).

Score	Content
4.0	Students will be able to determine whether various equations in two variables are linear and explain the reasons why or why not.
3.5	In addition to score 3.0 performance, partial success at score 4.0 content
3.0	Students will be able to graph linear relationships and compute and interpret the slope, midpoint, and distance between a given set of ordered pairs.
2.5	No major errors or omissions regarding score 2.0 content, and partial success at score 3.0 content
2.0	Students will be able to explain the basic process for graphing linear relationships. Students will be able to recognize, recall, or compute solutions to basic linear equations such as: <ul><li>The points (–2,–1) and (2,7) form a line that will cross the x axis at –1.5 and the y axis at 3.</li><li>The midpoint between (–1,2) and (3,–6) is (1,2).</li><li>The slope of the following ordered pairs is 2: (–4,–5) (–2,–1) (0,3) (2,7).</li></ul> Students will be able to recognize or recall basic terminology such as slope, midpoint, y intercept, x intercept, and linear equation.
1.5	Partial success at score 2.0 content, but major errors or omissions regarding score 3.0 content
1.0	With help, partial success at score 2.0 content and score 3.0 content
0.5	With help, partial success at score 2.0 content, but not at score 3.0 content
0.0	Even with help, no success

Figure 7.4: Scale for a mental procedure.

In figure 7.4, the instructional objective in score 3.0 involves the skill of graphing linear relationships and computing the slope, midpoint, and distance between a given set of ordered pairs, as well as the x and y intercepts. This is a fairly complex skill with a number of interacting steps. Score 2.0 content states that students will be able to describe the basic process for graphing linear relationships. This does not mean that students can execute the skill with fluency, but it does mean that students have a general understanding of the procedure. The score 2.0 content also requires students to demonstrate the ability to graph very simple problems involving ordered pairs and quickly compute the midpoint, slope, distance between two points, x intercept and y intercept. Finally, at this level, students can recognize or recall the general meaning of terms like *slope, midpoint,* y *intercept,* x *intercept,* and *linear equation.* Score 4.0 content goes beyond graphing linear equations by requiring students to reason from the equation to the type of relationship it reflects.

Planning for Score 2.0 Mental Procedure Content

With some notable exceptions, introductory lessons for mental procedures have the same elements as introductory lessons for information. Students are typically organized in small groups of two or three. When introducing score 2.0 content for mental procedures, a teacher will still help students preview the content. This might be a simple matter of asking students what they already know about linear equations, or using a partially completed outline as an introductory graphic organizer. Previewing for mental procedures is the same as previewing for information.

Chunking and scaffolding when introducing score 2.0 content for mental procedures must be done much more thoughtfully than is necessary with information. This is because the steps involved in a procedure either must be done in a specific order or are much more efficient if executed in a particular order. Therefore, a collaborative team engaged in lesson design would think through how the sequence of steps might be initially presented to students. For example, a collaborative team might identify the following sequence for the skill of graphing linear equations:

1. Plot each ordered pair on the graph.

2. Draw a line through the points. If you have plotted the points correctly, the line should be a straight line.

3. Once you have drawn a straight line, you can compute the midpoint by performing the following steps . . .

4. You can then compute the distance between two points by doing the following . . .

5. You can compute the slope by doing the following . . .

6. Make sure the line crosses both the x axis and the y axis. If it doesn't, extend the line so that it does.

7. Once you have a straight line that crosses the x axis and the y axis, you can compute the x intercept and the y intercept by . . .

Although providing a set of steps like these is certainly formulaic, it does provide an understandable introduction for graphing linear equations. With practice over time, students will shape the procedure into a more streamlined version of their own. However, when introducing a mental procedure, a clear initial model like the example can be very helpful.

The model also provides a blueprint to the teacher for the chunks he or she might use. In this case, each step might be a separate chunk of content. The teacher would first demonstrate a step and then have students try that step in their small groups using a different problem. The teacher introduces important terms while demonstrating the steps. Students then independently try the step the teacher has modeled.

In some cases, a collaborative team might decide that a procedure is too complex to be introduced all at once. In the example, a collaborative team might decide that the steps for computing the midpoint and the distance between two points might be initially left out and added later as students practice the procedure.

As with informational knowledge, students process the content in each chunk within their interaction groups. With procedural knowledge, group members share their experiences with the step they just tried on their own, identifying confusion or questions they might have. Interaction groups would try to address confusion and questions on their own before going to the teacher for assistance.

Teachers can also use elaboration when introducing procedural knowledge. Elaboration should occur after teachers have presented all scaffolded chunks and students have processed them. To elaborate on what students have just learned, the teacher might present a new graphing problem to the entire class. As the teacher again walks students through the various steps of the procedure, he or she might pose questions that require students to go beyond what was presented in the chunks. For example, the teacher might pose the elaborative question, "What would you know about a linear equation if it did not cross the x axis?"

Requiring students to represent new knowledge in linguistic and nonlinguistic ways can also be applied to procedural content. Students might be asked to describe in their own words the process of graphing a linear equation using a set of ordered pairs. Or students might be asked to construct a flow chart that represents the steps involved in graphing a linear equation.

Finally, an introductory lesson involving procedural knowledge can conclude with students answering reflection questions like the following:

- What steps are the easiest for you?
- What steps cause the greatest confusion for you?

Planning for Score 3.0 Mental Procedure Content

With mental procedures, score 3.0 content typically requires students to execute a procedure independently and with relative ease. This does not occur automatically. In fact, learning a new procedure involves identifiable stages. During the first stage, the learner is aware of how the skill works but is not really able to do it. Providing students with this general sense of the new procedure is the basic goal of introductory lessons. During the next stage, the learner begins to actually execute the procedure, but he or she must think about it consciously while doing so. Many errors are made during this phase as the learner tries to adapt the procedure to his or her particular needs and style. During the final phase, the learner develops the procedure to a level at which he or she can execute it with little conscious thought or can do it automatically with no conscious thought. This final stage is sometimes referred to as the *autonomous phase*, and reaching the autonomous phase requires practice. Unfortunately, there are some misconceptions surrounding the use of practice in the classroom.

Perhaps the most prominent misconception about practice originated with a misunderstanding of the theory of constructivism, which states that learning is an active constructive process in which students generate their unique understanding of content. According to cognitive psychologists Anderson, Reder, & Simon (1995), "One can readily agree with one part of the constructivist claim: that learning must be an active process" (p. 11). However, they go on to warn that the principle is sometimes overgeneralized to mean that structured practice somehow violates the principle of constructivism. Practice is essential to learning both mental and psychomotor procedural knowledge.

Another misconception regarding practice is that simply having students work through a number of problems or tasks that involve the skill qualifies as effective practice. In fact, there are a number of considerations for teams to address if practice is to be effective (Institute of Education Sciences, National Center for Education Research, 2007).

A first consideration is how teachers will integrate worked and nonworked examples. As students engage in practice, they should be exposed to alternated worked and nonworked examples. This is called "interleaving" (Institute of Education Sciences, National Center for Education Research, 2007). For example, during a practice session, a teacher might present students with ten problems, five of which would be worked for the students as examples of correct ways to address the problem, and five that would not be solved. Intuitively, it might seem that having students work through all ten problems on their own is better practice, but interleaving worked problems with examples students must solve themselves is a more effective approach.

How to ask students to analyze their own thinking is a second consideration. This can be done in the context of interleaving. While students are engaged in one of the nonworked problems, the teacher might ask one or more students to "think aloud," that is, to explain the thought processes that lead them from step to step. Additionally, the teacher might ask students to explain causal relationships inherent in the skill they are practicing. Questions that stimulate this type of thinking include, "Why did x have to be done before y? What would have happed if you did x instead of y? Why is it important that you do x as opposed to y?"

A third consideration is how to space practice sessions. Intuitively, it seems like practice sessions should be spaced closely together. This is not necessarily the case (Institute for Educational Sciences, National Center for Educational Research, 2007). A more serious problem than spacing practice sessions too far apart is to space them too close together. Ideally, at first students engage in practice sessions spaced rather close together, but then they experience increasingly longer intervals of time between practice sessions. In general, teachers should ensure that students practice important skills, strategies, and processes several weeks after initially presenting them, and then again several months after that.

The work of collaborative teams in planning lessons to help students reach score 3.0 status for mental procedures is quite clear: teams must design worked and nonworked examples, construct activities to help students analyze their own thinking, and set up an appropriate practice schedule.

Planning for Score 4.0 Mental Procedure Content

Score 4.0 content for mental procedures requires students to apply the mental procedure in very different contexts from those presented in class. In the case of the scale in figure 7.4, students are asked to discriminate between linear equations and nonlinear equations and defend their conclusions. This goes beyond graphing an equation; it represents a new context for the knowledge they have acquired at the score 3.0 level. Collaborative teams first generate a series of equations, some of which are linear and some of which are nonlinear, and students then use these equations to demonstrate their score 4.0 competence.

Summary of Lesson Study for Mental Procedures

To engage in lesson study for mental procedures, collaborative teams design introductory lessons for score 2.0 content that have some of the same components as introductory lessons for score 2.0 informational content; however, scaffolding is more critical to the lesson. Also, chunks are composed of steps or sets of steps in the procedure. Students independently try these steps and then discuss them within their interaction group. Lesson design for score 3.0 procedural content is quite different. It focuses on a series of practice sessions that allow students to reach a level of proficiency at which they can perform the procedure autonomously. Lesson design for score 4.0 content involves designing tasks that require students to utilize the procedure in ways not directly addressed in class.

Lesson Study for Psychomotor Procedures

Psychomotor procedures can be organized into the same two categories as mental procedures: processes and skills. As described previously in chapter 5, processes are complex procedures that usually include complex combination procedures, simple combination procedures, and foundational procedures. As is the case with mental procedures, instructional objectives for psychomotor procedures are usually written at the skill level. Consider the scale in figure 7.5.

Score	Content
4.0	Students will be able to adapt their swing to differing speeds of a pitch.
3.5	In addition to score 3.0 performance, partial success at score 4.0 content
3.0	Students will be able to hit a baseball by starting hip rotation when the ball is about halfway to the plate, keeping their eyes on the ball and swinging the bat without dropping the back elbow.
2.5	No major errors or omissions regarding score 2.0 content, and partial success at score 3.0 content
2.0	Students will be able to explain the basic process for hitting a baseball. Students will be able to demonstrate a stance in which the feet are about shoulder-width apart, back elbow is up, and the bat is perpendicular to the ground. Students will be able to recognize or recall basic terminology such as *hip rotation, follow through, timing,* and *eye on the ball.*
1.5	Partial success at score 2.0 content, but major errors or omissions regarding score 3.0 content
1.0	With help, partial success at score 2.0 content and score 3.0 content
0.5	With help, partial success at score 2.0 content, but not at score 3.0 content
0.0	Even with help, no success

Figure 7.5: Scale for a psychomotor procedure.

In figure 7.5, score 3.0 focuses on the skill of hitting a baseball using a specific procedure. Score 2.0 addresses a basic understanding of how to perform that skill. At the score 2.0 level, students are obtaining an initial understanding of how to execute the skill. At the score 4.0 level, students can apply the skill in novel situations. Specifically, they can adapt the procedure to different speeds of a pitch.

Planning for Score 2.0 Psychomotor Procedure Content

Introductory lessons for psychomotor procedures follow the same pattern as introductory lessons for score 2.0 mental procedures. Students are typically organized in small groups of two or three. The teacher helps students preview the content using strategies such as asking students what they already know about hitting a baseball.

Again, teachers must chunk and scaffold score 2.0 procedure content much more thoughtfully than with information. Collaborative teams engaged in lesson design must start by thinking through the sequence of steps in which the elements of the psychomotor procedure might be initially presented to students. For example, a collaborative team might identify the following sequence of actions to present to students:

1. Establish your stance, first making sure that your feet are about shoulder-width apart.

2. Next make sure that your back elbow is held high and is parallel to the ground. Also make sure that you are holding the bat tightly and it is perpendicular to the ground.

3. Carefully watch the pitch, but don't start your hip rotation until the ball is about half way to the plate.

4. Keeping your eye on the ball, decide whether the pitch is going to be in the strike zone.

5. If the ball is in the strike zone, swing using your wrists, keeping your eye on the ball all the way through your swing.

As with mental procedures, the teacher demonstrates each step in the process, introduces terms when appropriate, and engages students in trying the steps on their own. In this example, each student in class would have a bat, but students might have to imagine a ball being pitched. Once again, students process the content in each chunk within their interaction groups. Group members then share their experiences with the step they just tried on their own, identify any confusion or questions they might have, attempt to resolve the issues within their group, and finally seek the help of their teacher if they are unable to resolve the issues on their own.

Teachers can also employ elaboration after students have processed all of the scaffolded chunks. As the teacher again walks students through the various steps of the procedure, he or she might pose questions that require students to go beyond what was presented in the chunks. For example, an elaborative question posed to students might be, "How would you have to modify this process if the pitcher was very fast in his delivery?"

Teachers can also ask students to represent a newly introduced psychomotor procedure in linguistic and nonlinguistic ways. Teachers might ask students to describe in their own words the process of hitting a baseball. Or they might ask students to sketch the steps involved.

Finally, an introductory lesson can conclude with students answering reflection questions like the following:

- What steps are the easiest for you?
- What steps are problematic for you? Why?

Planning for Score 3.0 Psychomotor Procedure Content

As with mental procedures, to get to a score 3.0 level for psychomotor procedures, students must engage in a series of practice sessions that span a number of classes. Again, collaborative teams must address a number of considerations when designing these practice sessions.

A first consideration is how practice sessions will address specific steps as opposed to the entire procedure. Since psychomotor procedures involve sets of physical movement that commonly are not used together in everyday life, a collaborative team might decide to devote some parts of a practice session to a single step. For example, a good part of the initial practice sessions might be devoted to hip rotation in isolation since it is a movement not commonly used outside of a sports environment. The teams might establish focused practice for this movement alone.

As with mental procedures, a second consideration is how to engage students in analyzing their own performance by asking questions such as, "Why is it important to wait to start your hip rotation?" A third consideration for collaborative teams is how to space practice sessions.

Planning for Score 4.0 Psychomotor Procedure Content

At the score 4.0 level, students can execute the target procedure in unusual situations. In the example, students are able to adapt the procedure for hitting a baseball to different pitch speeds. The task of collaborative teams is to design situations in which students can demonstrate use of the procedure beyond the 3.0 level. This might be as straightforward as providing opportunities for students to face pitches of different speeds.

Summary of Lesson Study for Psychomotor Procedures

To engage in lesson study for psychomotor procedures, collaborative teams create introductory lessons that follow the same format as score 2.0 introductory lessons for mental procedures, with the exception that students physically execute each step before they discuss the step in their interaction groups. Practice sessions that help students reach the autonomous stage implicit in score 3.0 require the same considerations for psychomotor procedures as do mental procedures. Similarly, score 4.0 tasks for psychomotor procedures must be designed in such a way that students can demonstrate use of the skill in ways not addressed in class.

Observing Lessons in Action

Collaborative teams in a PLC should observe and revise their lessons over time. Instructional rounds are one tool teams can use to examine the impact of instructional practices developed through the lesson study process.

Instructional rounds have been used by administrators, teacher supervisors, and instructional coaches "to focus on a common problem of practice that cuts across all levels of the system" (City, Elmore, Fiarman, & Teitel, 2009, p. 5). In Bob's work with schools and districts, he has found that instructional rounds are more effective when conducted by teams of teachers and used in the following ways. For a complete discussion of the nature and purpose of instructional rounds, see Marzano et al. (in press).

A Nonevaluative Approach

Instructional rounds are intended to allow members of collaborative teams to examine the effectiveness of lessons designed by the team and to compare their individual instructional practices with those they observe in the classrooms they visit. It is the collective reflection and discussion at the end of instructional rounds that provide the chief benefit. Rounds typically are not used to provide feedback to the teacher being observed; however, they can be used for this purpose if the teacher being observed so desires. In that event, the observing group of teachers summarizes their observations and makes their comments available to the observed teacher. In all cases, the observed teacher should demonstrate one of the lessons developed by the collaborative team during lesson design.

Conducting Rounds

Groups conducting rounds are usually small in numbers—three to five members—and a lead teacher, team leader, or instructional coach who has the respect of the team and serves as a facilitator. Administrators may also facilitate rounds, but it should be made clear from the outset that their purpose is not to evaluate the teachers being observed.

On the day of the observation, the teacher demonstrating the lesson should advise students that other teachers will be visiting their classroom and explain the purpose behind the visit—so that teachers in the school can learn from one another just as students learn from one another. When the observer teachers enter a classroom, they quietly move to some portion of the classroom that does not disrupt the flow of instruction, typically at the back or side of the classroom. They observe what is occurring and make notes regarding use of specific instructional strategies. At the end of the observation, the team of observers exits the classroom, making sure to thank the observed teacher and the students.

Debriefing Rounds

After each round, members of the observing team convene to reflect on their experiences in a round-robin format in which each member comments on what he or she observed. The leader of the rounds starts by reviewing the purpose of the discussion and ground rules for dialogue. Such rules might include the following:

- Do not offer suggestions to the observed teacher unless he or she explicitly asks for feedback.
- Do not share comments made during the debriefing with anyone outside of the team.

As observer teachers take turns commenting on what they saw in a particular classroom, it is helpful to use a "pluses and deltas" format. Each participant begins by noting the positive things (pluses) he or she saw in the classroom. For example, an observer might comment on how well managed the classroom was and the variety of strategies the teacher used to check for understanding. Next, the observer speculates as to what produced the positive outcome. For example, the observer teacher might postulate that the classroom appeared well managed because the students were clearly aware of specific routines they were to use, such as raising their hands when asking a question and how to move from one activity to another.

Finally, the observer mentions some questions or concerns (deltas) he or she has about the teacher's use of strategies. For example, the observer might make the comment, "I'm not sure why the teacher stayed so long with students when they answered a question incorrectly. I think that slowed things down too much." At this point, other observers might add their thoughts about the issue.

Each observer teacher shares his or her pluses and deltas. The process is the same for each observed teacher. An observer teacher can always opt not to share his or her analysis with the group for any observation.

Finally, the observer teachers make specific comments about the structure of the lesson. Once again, their primary focus is not on the teacher, but rather it is on the structure of the lesson that was designed by the collaborative team and executed by the teacher. Members critique the specific elements of the lesson.

Summarizing Experiences

Instructional rounds end with the observer teachers addressing both their individual practice and the effectiveness of the lesson developed by the team. Questions might include:

- What instructional practices will I continue to use because I saw other teachers employing them effectively?

- What instructional strategies that I currently use will I re-examine?

- What strategies have I not used but will now attempt because I saw them effectively used by other teachers?

- What part of our team-developed lesson plan worked well?

- What part of our team-developed lesson plan did not work as well as we had hoped and what might we do to change it?

For example, an observer teacher might decide, "As a result of what I saw today, I'm going to continue calling on students randomly when I ask questions. Other teachers seem to have success with this strategy; however, I'm going to re-examine how long I stay with students with probing questions when they've answered a question incorrectly. It seems to slow things down too much if you stay with students too long. Finally, I've got some new ideas about routines I need to implement with my students."

The team members then summarize their reflections about the structure of the lesson and consider how they might improve the lesson. The team could then consider ways to improve the preview that address that issue.

Conclusion

Instructional rounds complement, but should not substitute for, the members of a collaborative team of teachers working together to examine evidence of student learning from common assessments and making inferences about the effectiveness of instruction based on that evidence. As Hattie (2009) emphasized, it is not merely reflecting about teaching that impacts student learning, but collective reflection by *teams* of teachers "*in light of evidence about their teaching*" (p. 239). Educators must ultimately shift the conversation from "What was taught?" or "How was it taught?" to the questions of "What was learned?" and "How can we use evidence of student learning to strengthen our professional practice?" (DuFour & Marzano, 2009, p. 62).

On the other hand, it is entirely possible that a teacher who was very effective in helping students learn at high levels is unable to articulate the specific strategies he or she used to get those results. Instructional rounds could be used not only to help team members identify those strategies, but also to help the teacher become more aware of his or her teaching. When done well, instructional rounds provide another opportunity for the collaboration and collective inquiry that drive continuous improvement in a PLC.

CHAPTER 8

Responding When Kids Don't Learn

[Highly effective schools] succeed where other schools fail because they ruthlessly organize themselves around one thing: helping students learn a great deal. This seems too simple an explanation, really. But, by focusing on student learning and then creating structures that support learning, these schools have drastically departed from the traditional organizational patterns of American schools.

—Karin Chenoweth

If there are certainties in education, one is that despite the best efforts of well-intentioned individual classroom teachers, some students will struggle to acquire the knowledge, skills, and dispositions those teachers work so hard to convey. A team of teachers can work conscientiously to create a guaranteed and viable curriculum, plan wonderful lessons, use varied instructional strategies, monitor learning in their classrooms on an ongoing basis, and develop valid and reliable assessments, only to find at the conclusion of the unit that some students did not learn. To say this is a perennial problem understates the issue. It does not merely happen over the course of a year or two but typically will occur at the conclusion of each unit, if not each lesson. How does a collaborative team of teachers respond when, at the end of a carefully designed and executed unit, some students have mastered the objective and others have not? In this chapter we examine how a professional learning community addresses this challenge in a systematic way.

A Schoolwide Response to Students Who Do Not Learn

The question of how schools have traditionally responded when students are not learning can be considered from two very different perspectives. On the one hand, it can be argued that schools have been tireless in their efforts to address the problem and have been willing to pursue multiple strategies for improving student learning. Consider just some of the ideas that have been implemented in different schools in an effort to raise student achievement:

- Adopting new curriculum programs and/or new textbooks

- Scripting lessons so that all teachers will provide the same instruction with fidelity

- Changing the structure of schools by breaking big high schools into smaller schools or constantly reconfiguring the grade levels to be served on specific campuses

- Changing schedules—moving from 50-minute periods to 90-minute periods

- Converting elementary schools from self-contained classrooms in which individual teachers provide primary instruction to the same group of students in all core subject areas to departmentalized grade levels in which students have a different teacher for each subject

- Creating additional levels or tracks and placing students who struggle in lower tracks.

- Changing school policies such as applying stricter dress codes, requiring school uniforms, or moving to single-sex schools

- Providing rewards—movie tickets, iPods, money—for students who do learn

- Providing rewards—merit pay bonuses—for teachers whose students score higher on standardized tests

- Raising the requirements to enter the teaching profession
  or making it easier to enter the teaching profession

In fact, between 1987 and 1997, *Phi Delta Kappan* reported 361 different good ideas for improving student achievement (Carpenter, 2000), and virtually all of them have been tried at different schools throughout the United States. The list of good ideas has certainly grown since Carpenter's study. In a recent synthesis of over eight hundred meta-analyses of factors alleged to impact student achievement, John Hattie (2009) found a plethora of proposals that had been put forth to improve schools. He noted this fascinating discovery:

> Many of the most debated issues are the ones with the least effects. It is a powerful question to ask why such issues as class size, tracking, retention (that is, holding a student back a grade), school choice, summer schools, and school uniforms command such heated discussion and strong claims. Such cosmetic or "coat of paint" reforms are too common. (p. 33)

We believe there are two answers to Hattie's question of why schools so often invest so much effort and energy into structural changes that have little impact on student achievement. The first is that structural changes are easy to make. You can change the structure by fiat. The second reason for the popularity of structural tweaking is because it allows educators to convey the illusion of change. Reorganizing and restructuring can create a false sense that you are actually doing something productive. Changing the structure or moving boxes around on the organizational chart won't change the culture and too often serve as strategies for avoiding the brutal facts (Collins, 2009).

One of the most persistent brutal facts in education is the disconnect between the proclaimed commitment to ensure all students learn and the lack of a thoughtful, coordinated, and systematic response when some students do not learn in spite of the best efforts of their individual classroom teacher. Despite all the talk of educational reform, what happens to a student when he or she struggles to acquire a skill or concept and continues to depend almost exclusively on the teacher to whom that student is assigned. Despite this glaring misalignment between purpose and practice, in most schools educators continue to invest in "coat of paint" structural changes that have little impact on student achievement rather than addressing this fundamental cultural problem in a meaningful way.

In working with tens of thousands of educators over the past decade, we find that educators themselves readily acknowledge that their schools have no set plan or process for responding to students who struggle. They agree that some teachers in their schools will:

- Allow students to retake a test or quiz, and others will not

- Contact parents to keep them informed of their child's progress and solicit their help, and others will not

- Work with students before and after school to provide additional support for learning, and others will not or cannot

- Return student work and require a student to make changes until it meets a certain standard, and others will simply assign a failing grade to the initial work

In short, they agree that their schools are playing an educational lottery with students—that the response to students when they struggle will depend primarily if not exclusively on the randomness of the teacher to whom they are assigned. They laugh knowingly (and sheepishly) when we share stories of teachers who appeal to the principal or the counselor to make sure that their own children are not assigned to particular teachers. This kind of insider trading information could result in prison time on Wall Street, but in the world of education it is routinely considered a professional perk.

If the improvement strategies schools implement are to move beyond the cosmetic reforms decried by Hattie to address more substantive issues, those reforms must begin to impact both the practice of individual teachers in their classrooms *and* the collective practice of the school when students struggle. Any school or district that claims its mission is to help all students learn at high levels—as most do—must certainly be prepared to address the questions of what do we want our students to learn and how will we know when they have learned it. It is equally imperative, however, for those schools and districts to address the crucial questions of how will we respond when students don't learn and how can we enrich and extend the learning for those who are proficient.

Response to Intervention: Is It the Solution?

With the passage of the Individuals with Disabilities Education Improvement Act (IDEIA) in 2004, schools and districts were called upon to create a more structured and timely approach to responding to students who experience difficulty in school. This response to intervention (RTI) approach was to be based on high-quality initial instruction for every student in every classroom, continuous monitoring of student learning through formative assessment processes that provided timely information about each student's progress toward desired goals, and tiered systems of intervention that provided extra time and increasingly intensive support for students who continued to struggle. Very importantly, RTI asked educators to take collective responsibility for each student's learning and work collaboratively to ensure that learning (International Reading Association Commission on RTI, 2009).

The basic idea of RTI—present good initial instruction, assess frequently, provide prompt assistance for struggling students to catch learning problems before they become more serious, and follow up relentlessly—just makes sense. Furthermore, RTI reflects the big ideas that drive the PLC process—an intense focus on the learning of each student, a collaborative and collective effort to ensure that learning, and ongoing analysis of evidence of each student's learning to better meet his or her needs. PLC and RTI seem to be a perfect fit. What could go wrong? The answer to that question, unfortunately, is "A lot!"

Mistaken Approaches to Response to Intervention

Following are ten common mistakes schools and districts continue to make as they address the challenge of providing support for students who are not learning.

1. RTI becomes an appendage to traditional schooling practices rather than a catalyst for the cultural changes effective intervention requires.

   If teachers define their role as teaching rather than ensuring student learning, a system of intervention can provide yet another reason that classroom teachers avoid taking responsibility for student learning. In the wrong school culture, teachers can assume, "I taught it, and they didn't get it, so let the system of intervention deal with them." If teachers continue to work in isolation—if what a student is taught, when content is taught, and how learning is assessed is left to the discretion of the individual classroom teacher—a system of intervention intended to promote a collective effort to raise student achievement will be ineffective. If educators continue to view assessments merely as a tool for assigning grades rather than a process for addressing student needs and improving professional practice, intervention will have little impact on enhancing student learning. Effective intervention must be integrated within the context of a guaranteed curriculum, informative assessments, and a process of continuous improvement (IRA Commission on RTI, 2009). Simply put, to implement systematic interventions successfully, "a school must not only provide its staff with a new set of 'tools' to help students learn, but must also help educators develop a new way of thinking about their roles and responsibilities" (Buffum, Mattos, & Weber, in press).

2. RTI is viewed as a checklist to complete or a program to be purchased to comply with regulations rather than an ongoing process to improve student learning.

If educators believe that RTI simply requires completing the steps on a checklist, purchasing new curriculum, or assigning students who struggle to a computer-based program of learning in order to meet the stipulations of new regulations, the schools will fail to develop effective systems of intervention. As leading authors on RTI conclude, "If there is one thing that traditional special education has taught us, it's that staying compliant does not necessarily lead to improved student learning—in fact, the opposite is more often the case" (Buffum, Mattos, & Weber, 2010, p. 13).

3. RTI is reactive rather than proactive.

We have seen intervention plans that have no process for identifying and supporting students until they have failed a grading period. This "wait to fail" strategy offers the equivalent of an educational autopsy rather than the ongoing monitoring of student learning that RTI is intended to offer.

4. RTI does not provide additional time or differentiated support for learning.

Intervention plans that remove students from reading instruction to provide them with reading instruction may be offering students teaching in a different setting, but they are not offering additional time for learning. Plans that simply repeat the same instructional strategies that have already proven to be ineffective for particular students might provide those students with more time for learning, but "more of the same" is not effective intervention.

5. RTI invites students to access available interventions.

   When educators claim that they have addressed the challenge of a systematic intervention by inviting students who
   need help to "stop in" before or after school for assistance if
   they are so inclined, they fail to grasp the meaning of either
   systematic or *intervention*.

6. RTI is based on seat time rather than proficiency.

   When students are assigned to intervention for a designated length of time (for example, nine weeks or a semes-
   ter) rather than until they demonstrate proficiency, the
   focus of intervention becomes ensuring students complete
   the allotted time rather than ensuring that they learn.
   Again, if educators concentrate on compliance rather than
   results, intervention will be ineffective.

7. RTI focuses on symptoms rather than causes.

   When educators assign students to intervention because
   they are "failing language arts," they are responding to a
   symptom; but without greater clarity regarding what is
   causing the failure, they will be unable to intervene effectively. They are tantamount to a doctor prescribing a specific antidote based solely on the knowledge that a patient
   is experiencing chest pain. Chest pain can be caused by a
   myriad of factors—from heartburn to a heart attack. To
   treat the symptom effectively, more precise information is
   required. Effective intervention will be based on in-depth
   knowledge of the specific skill the student is lacking and
   the most effective strategies for helping the student acquire
   that skill.

8. RTI does not provide the channels of communication
   essential to effective intervention.

   A collective and systematic approach to intervention
   requires effective communication between all those
   who contribute to the intervention process—classroom

teachers, collaborative teams, special education teachers, instructional coaches, counselors, and school administrators. If key school personnel are unable to articulate the desired outcome for the student, the specific steps of the intervention plan, the responsibilities of all those who provide the intervention, how student progress will be monitored, and the standard the student must achieve to no longer require the service, the intervention process will be ineffective. The process must ensure that all of the respective parties are provided with ongoing information regarding the specific needs and progress of individual students.

9. RTI assigns the least-skilled adults to work with the students most in need of expert teaching.

In many schools, students who struggle are assigned to well-intentioned people who lack the pedagogical skill and content expertise to resolve the students' learning difficulties. Too often, intervention is provided by parent volunteers, paraprofessionals, teacher assistants, or special education teachers who may be trained in particular learning disabilities but lack an in-depth knowledge of the progression of skills a particular subject area requires. As Richard Allington, the former president of the International Reading Association, laments, when schools assign people without expertise to the hardest kids to teach, "you penalize children for the rest of their lives because of your decision," yet routinely "no one gets worse or less instruction than the kids who need it most" (Rebora, 2010).

10. RTI is viewed as a special education program.

The most common mistake educators are making regarding RTI is viewing it as an extension of special education. RTI was specifically intended to address general education by strengthening classroom instruction and providing systematic intervention for *all* students in order to limit the

number of students assigned to special education to those
with physical or mental disabilities.

When done well, special education programs serve a vital
purpose in our schools. Special education not only gives
access to public schooling to students who in the past
were denied such access, but it also provides the additional time and focused support to help those students
acquire essential knowledge and skills. In many schools,
however, the only way any student could get access to
additional help was to place them in special education.
Students were assigned to special education programs not
because of physical or mental disabilities, but because they
were experiencing difficulty. As a result, well-intentioned
special education personnel often struggled to provide
the effective services their programs were designed to
provide (President's Commission on Excellence in Special
Education, 2002).

If schools consider RTI a special education initiative to get
more students into special education faster, it will do far
more harm than good. It will merely reinforce rather than
eliminate the artificial gap that often exists between general education and special education teachers. If general
education teachers assume that students who experience
difficulty have some neurological difficulty, and it falls to
special education teachers to solve their problem, intervention will be ineffective.

Effective Systems of Intervention

We offer the following ten recommendations for any school
attempting to create a systematic process to respond to students
who experience difficulty in their learning.

1. The plan of intervention must begin by providing all students with access to effective instruction each day.

No plan of intervention can compensate for consistently weak and ineffective teaching. At the same time the school is attempting to provide students with the time, support, and information they need to improve their learning, the school must also provide its educators with the time, support, and information they need to become more effective in meeting their professional responsibilities.

2. The plan of intervention must be proactive rather than reactive.

The school should have a process for assessing both the proficiency levels and the unique needs of students as they enter the school in order to provide a proactive response to students. In too many schools there is no such process, and months can go by before a student's difficulty becomes apparent to anyone other than the individual classroom teacher. Every day a student is in a downward spiral makes it more difficult to resolve his or her problems. If the school is to respond, steps must be taken to ensure educators beyond the classroom teacher are aware of the student's difficulties. The simple question, "Which of your students will need us most?" should be asked by receiving schools when students make the transition from one school to the next. The same question should be asked by grade-level or course-specific teams as students advance through the curriculum of a single school.

3. The plan of intervention must rely on an assessment process that provides multiple people with frequent and timely information about the learning of each student.

We have attempted to make the case that gathering evidence of student learning by individual teachers in their classrooms and by teams of teachers through their collaborative teams is essential to effective teaching. Ongoing information about each student's learning is the fuel that drives the intervention process, and a frequent, effective,

high-quality assessment process is necessary to provide
that information.

4. The plan of intervention must be multilayered with time
   and support for learning as variables rather than constants.

   In most schools, year after year and unit by unit the
   amount of time students are provided to learn a concept
   will be the same for the most accomplished students in
   the class as it is for the students who struggle the most.
   The same is true for the level of the support that individual
   students receive from their teacher. This is not the fault of
   the teacher. There are only so many minutes of instruction
   available. An individual teacher does not have the discretion to convert a fifty-minute class period into a seventy-
   five-minute period. Furthermore, if that teacher devotes
   considerable classroom time and personal attention to a
   few students who struggle, his or her efforts to leave no
   child behind may have an adverse impact on the learning of
   other students in the class. Effective plans of intervention
   will ensure that students receive additional time and support for learning in ways that do not remove those students
   from new direct instruction. Furthermore, if the current
   level of time and support a student is receiving is not
   resulting in his or her learning, the school plan will include
   additional tiers that provide the student with even more
   time and more intensive support. Time and support will be
   regarded as variables rather than constants, as resources
   that can be increased based on the needs of individual
   students.

5. The plan of intervention will be directive rather than
   invitational.

   An effective plan of intervention will not invite students
   to devote additional time to their learning or to utilize
   additional layers of support—it will require them to do
   so. Students most in need of help in order to succeed are

often the least likely to pursue it. So the school must have a process in place that assigns students to intervention just as it has a process that assigns them to a mathematics class or lunch. The entire atmosphere of the school will be warm but demanding, staffed by educators who "model and insist on a culture of achievement, equity, and mutual respect.... They insist that children try hard, encourage others to try hard, and do their best every day" (Ross, Bondy, Gallingane, & Hambacher, 2008, p. 143).

6. The plan of intervention will be fluid and flexible.

Rather than assigning students into specific programs for designated periods of time, the plan of intervention should respond immediately to an individual student who struggles and provide additional time and support only until that student demonstrates proficiency. Unlike special education programs where it is difficult and time consuming for a student to be identified as eligible for services, and then unlikely that the student will ever be found to no longer need the services, students flow in and out of the intervention as needed. Furthermore, although sequential steps of increasing support may be included in the plan, the school has the option of accelerating or skipping those steps for students who are experiencing significant difficulties.

7. The plan of intervention would be characterized by specificity and precision regarding the needs of a particular student.

The assessment process utilized by the school should identify the specific area of difficulty a student is experiencing and provide insights as to how that difficulty can be addressed. A student who is assigned to intervention because "he is not doing well in mathematics" will not be as well served as a student in a system that can stipulate, "He is having difficulty adding and subtracting two-digit integers."

8. The plan of intervention should address the needs of both nonintentional and intentional non-learners.

Some students who are not succeeding are making a good faith effort to acquire the intended knowledge and skills, but are struggling despite their efforts. Other students simply are unwilling to put forth the effort needed to be successful. The former need interventions that provide them with intensive tutorial support by effective teachers who can identify the problem the student is experiencing and can provide instruction to help overcome that problem. The latter need interventions that ensure they complete their work according to an acceptable standard. If that level of support fails to impact their effort, the student and family may need noninstructional services to determine why he or she is engaging in unproductive behavior. The best plans of intervention do not use a single strategy to address the needs of these very different students but will provide interventions that reflect and respond to their respective needs.

9. The plan of intervention should be systematic.

When something is done systematically, it happens according to a defined plan that is arranged in an organized, methodical, step-by-step process. A systematic plan of intervention represents the antithesis of the random, discretionary, haphazard way in which schools have traditionally responded to students who experience difficulty. Teachers and administrators work together to identify and implement specific trigger points for specific interventions. They define each step in the intervention plan and clarify roles and responsibilities for all staff. Particular people will be designated to oversee the process, and everyone on the staff will be aware of who those people are. These intervention leaders will be provided with time to collaborate on a regular basis and will be responsible for (1) identifying which students need intervention according to the criteria established by the school, (2) ensuring appropriate intervention takes place for any student who requires it, and (3) monitoring the impact of the intervention on an ongoing basis to determine which students need the next step in the intervention plan and which students no longer require intervention (DuFour, DuFour, Eaker, & Many, 2010).

Effective plans of intervention will put an end to the educational lottery traditionally experienced by students when they experience academic difficulty:

> When a school creates a plan for systematic interventions it is able to *guarantee* students that they will be given additional time and support if they struggle, to *guarantee* parents that their children will receive this support in a timely and directive way regardless of the teacher to whom they are assigned, and to *guarantee* individual teachers that they are not alone when it comes to resolving the problems their students may experience. The entire staff realizes that there is a collective and coordinated effort to assist students. (DuFour, DuFour, Eaker, & Many, 2010. p. 224)

10. The plan of intervention will be embedded in a culture of high expectations, collaboration, and continuous improvement.

    Because systematic intervention is intended to serve *all* students and not only students who routinely struggle, it helps destigmatize the need for intervention (Barber & Mourshed, 2007). An effective plan supports the student who has a problem grasping a calculus concept as well as the student who has difficulty in mastering multiplication tables.

    High-achieving students often fail to admit they are struggling because they are afraid they will be seen as

lacking the innate ability to succeed (Dweck, 2006). But
when schools create systematic interventions that serve all
students, educators convey what psychologist Carol Dweck
calls the high expectations of a "growth mindset"—the
belief that academic achievement is the result of sustained
effort rather than innate ability. The message that "You
have not learned *yet,* but you will," is very different than
the message, "You cannot learn because you are not smart
enough." The assumption that you must keep working until
you are successful is very different from the assumption
that you must learn within the allotted time. Systematic
intervention, done well, creates the challenging yet nurtur-
ing environment that helps students of all abilities develop
the growth mindset.

At this point it should be evident that RTI works best when
schools function as professional learning communities. As
Buffum et al. (in press) conclude in their excellent exami-
nation of effective systems of intervention, "Professional
learning communities create the schoolwide cultural and
structural foundation necessary to implement a highly
effective response to intervention program."

Enrichment in a Professional Learning Community

The fourth of the critical questions that members of a PLC consider is, "How will we enrich and extend the learning for students
who are proficient?" Once again, the response should be based on a
collective and systematic effort rather than left to chance. Here are
seven strategies being used by schools to address that important
question:

1. Provide students with the specific criteria they must
    achieve in order to demonstrate advanced proficiency.

    As we demonstrated in chapters 5 and 6, one of the most
    powerful ways that schools can help proficient students

extend their learning is to use proficiency scales that help students understand exactly what they must do and demonstrate to achieve advanced proficiency.

2. Build enrichment activities into each unit of instruction.

At Anne Fox Elementary School in Hanover Park, Illinois, and Highland Elementary School in Montgomery, Maryland, the master schedule is designed to provide each grade level with a block of time each day for enrichment and intervention. In planning each unit, the collaborative team at each grade level develops specific activities for students who demonstrate advanced proficiency on the common assessment at the end of the unit. One or more members of the team will work with those students during the intervention/enrichment block. The students do not receive new direct instruction but engage in activities created by the team to deepen their understanding of a skill or concept.

At Frost Middle School in Schaumburg, Illinois, and Bernice McNaughton High School in New Brunswick, Canada, teams plan for "redeployment" at the end of each unit. Students in the same course are redistributed to different teachers based on their level of proficiency at the end of the unit. Redeployment will typically last two or three days as some students receive intervention, proficient students practice their newly acquired skill, and highly proficient students engage in enrichment activities. Once again, the entire team plans for these different levels of support, and once again enrichment is intended to deepen students' understanding of a skill or concept rather than present new direct instruction. After several days of redeployment, students return to their "home" teacher, and the team begins the next unit of instruction.

Schools committed to enriching student learning will build time into the school day for enrichment and will call upon teams to work collaboratively to ensure that time is used well.

3. Provide students with access to more rigorous curriculum.

In schools that offer advanced curriculum, one way to enrich the learning of students is to provide more students with access to that curriculum. This is another manifestation of the concept of opportunity to learn that we presented in chapter 5. Students cannot learn at advanced levels if they are not given the opportunity to do so. At one point in its history, Adlai Stevenson High School in Lincolnshire, Illinois, excluded any student who had not scored in the top ten percent of the entering freshman class from access to curriculum that would allow the student to pursue college work in high school. The school changed its philosophy, removed barriers to its most rigorous curriculum, began to encourage students demonstrating proficiency in the standard curriculum to accept the challenge of the advanced curriculum, and provided time during the school day to provide those students with additional support to meet that challenge. The school increased student participation in its most advanced curriculum by over 1000 percent, yet had a higher percentage of its students earning honor grades on advanced placement exams than when it restricted access to that program to the elite few.

4. Allow participation in cocurricular programs.

Cocurricular programs provide another opportunity for enrichment, particularly at the middle and high school levels. Cinco Ranch High School in Katy, Texas, illustrates a commitment to enrich the learning of its students by providing them with multiple opportunities to apply their learning outside the traditional classroom. When students have the opportunity to participate on math teams, Junior Engineering Technical Society teams, and forensics teams, they can pursue their interests in a given subject. When they can demonstrate their learning in academic decathlons, history fairs, science Olympiads, model United

Nations programs, creative writing contests, music competitions, and future business leaders competitions, they can challenge themselves to reach high standards.

5. Provide the option of independent study related to the topic.

When students are able to demonstrate advanced proficiency on content that has yet to be taught, they benefit from the opportunity to pursue an independent study under the tutelage of a teacher rather than remaining in class to practice skills they have already mastered. A well-constructed independent study project can provide students with some of the deepest and most memorable learning they will experience in school.

6. Use students as tutors.

One very effective way to understand a concept or subject at a deeper level is to attempt teaching it to others. Advanced students can benefit from serving as tutors to other students. Bernice McNaughton High School has created a program to teach its advanced students to tutor others and uses those students as part of its intervention program.

7. Provide internships and mentorships.

Highly proficient students can benefit from serving as interns in a field that interests them or being provided with mentors from those fields. Adlai Stevenson High School has developed an active partnership with professionals in the area who offer internships and serve as mentors to Stevenson students.

But the Schedule Won't Let Us

We routinely work with school districts that declare their mission is to ensure all students will learn. Those same districts also readily acknowledge that if *all* students are to learn, some will need more time and support than others. Yet when asked if they are providing students who experience difficulty with additional time and support, they routinely answer they do not because "the schedule won't let us."

One exploration of schools and districts that have experienced dramatic gains in student achievement through a commitment to systematic intervention highlighted thirty-eight very different schools (DuFour, DuFour, Eaker, & Karhanek, 2010). They included urban, suburban, and rural schools; high- and low-minority populations; schools serving affluent areas and schools serving some of the poorest areas in the nation. They included elementary, middle, junior high, and high schools. They included small and big schools. They operated in different states and used very different schedules—six period days, seven period days, eight period days, nine period days, block schedules, modified block schedules, and very unique elementary schedules. What these schools had in common, however, was a commitment to creating a schedule that gave school personnel access to students who were experiencing difficulty in their learning during the school day. This additional time and support for learning occurred in ways that did not require students to miss new direct instruction.

Another commonality among these schools was that the percentage of students demonstrating advanced proficiency increased dramatically. Education is not a zero sum game, and the attention these schools gave to both intervention and enrichment benefitted students throughout the school. As Rick and his colleagues observed (DuFour, DuFour, Eaker, & Karhanek, 2010):

> When teachers work together to become so skillful in teaching a particular concept that even students who typically have difficulty can understand that concept, all students benefit. When students of all abilities and levels of performance have a place to turn for extra time and support if they experience initial difficulty in learning, all students benefit. A school culture that both stretches *and* supports students is a good place for all kids. (p. 215)

A school's schedule should be regarded as a tool to further priorities rather than an impediment to change. Our advice to educators is simple: your schedule is not a sacred document. If your current schedule does not allow you to provide students with something as essential to their academic success as extra time and support for learning through systematic intervention and enrichment, you should change it!

Conclusion

An analysis of the "world's best-performing school systems" concluded:

> The best school systems take the process of monitoring student learning and intervention inside schools, constantly evaluating student performance and constructing interventions to assist individual students in order to prevent them from falling behind. . . . By intervening quickly at the level of the individual student . . . [these systems] prevent early failure from compounding into long-term failure. (Barber & Mourshed, 2007, p. 38)

The most effective intervention will always begin at the classroom level with skillful teachers who are clear on the intended outcomes and the progression of learning required to achieve the outcomes, who are constantly gathering evidence of student learning through formative assessment processes, and who use that evidence to address the specific needs of individual students. Effective intervention must, however, include a schoolwide process that can identify students *by name and by need* and then provide them with timely, directive, precise, and systematic support to keep them moving forward with their learning.

.

CHAPTER 9

Leadership Is an Affair
of the Heart

Rational clarity does not always create the emotional
commitment that motivates a desired behavior. And
when emotional factors are not taken into account,
organizations fall short of their intended goals. . . .
Emotional influences shape attitudes and drive
behaviors as much as logical arguments and rational
influences.

—John R. Katzenbach and Zia Kahn

Throughout this book we have attempted to provide an explanation of how effective educational leaders—superintendents, principals, and teachers—implement powerful concepts and processes
in order to improve student learning. We have cited research, referenced correlations, and shared data. We have described these
leaders as results oriented, tight, and intensely focused on nondiscretionary goals. Any book on effective leadership, however,
must acknowledge that these same bottom-line leaders who hold
themselves and others accountable for providing tangible evidence
of improved student learning also appeal directly to the emotions
of those they lead.

Appealing to the emotions has been described as the "first . . . and
most important act of leadership" (Goleman, Boyatzis, & McKee,
2002, p. 5). Katzenbach and Kahn (2010) agree that effective leaders
appeal not only to the head through research and logic, but also to
the heart by connecting to the emotional needs of their people. As
a comprehensive study of leadership concluded, "Purely and simply,

exemplary leaders excel at improving performance because they pay great attention to the human heart" (Kouzes & Posner, 2010, p. 136).

One of the ways effective leaders appeal to the heart is through the use of stories (Gardner, 1993). The ability to reach people through stories has been called "the ultimate hallmark of world-class leaders" (Tichy, 1997, p. 173) and one of the most powerful strategies for influencing the thinking and behavior of others (Patterson et al., 2008). In this final chapter, we include both data and stories to illustrate the importance of leadership as an affair of the heart.

Leadership as a Love Affair

The best educational leaders are in love—in love with the work they do, with the purpose their work serves, and with the people they lead and serve. They are more prone to think of what they do as a calling or a cause rather than a job. The best leaders we have known at the district, school, and classroom level all demonstrate a palpable passion for a moral purpose, and it is that passion that helps them persevere when confronting the inevitable difficulties of attempting to bring about substantive change.

When Michael Fullan looked for examples of effective system-wide school improvement, he selected Sanger Unified School District near Fresno, California. Marcus Johnson, Sanger's superintendent and the 2011 American Association of School Administrator's National Superintendent of the Year, led the collective effort that brought the school district out of Program Improvement and created exemplary schools throughout the district. Johnson was fueled by the belief that quality education was the key that unlocked doors of opportunity to the predominantly poor Hispanic students served by the district. He rejected the idea that demographics determine destiny and rallied the staff around a mantra that came to be understood and acted on throughout the district: "Do not blame the kids." The district's academic performance index rose from 657 in 2004 to 805 in 2010. In 2004 only two of the fifteen schools in the district performed in the top half of the state when compared to similar schools, five scored in the bottom 10 percent, and three more were in the bottom 20 percent. By 2010 *all* of the schools in the district were in the top 30 percent of similar schools, nine were in the highest decile, and the district was performing significantly above the state's performance despite massive cuts in funding and a student population that had 78 percent of its members living in poverty.

Ed Rafferty, superintendent of Schaumburg District 54 in suburban Chicago, faced a different challenge—how to move a district of twenty-seven schools and more than 14,000 students from good to great. In 2006 he asked the board of education to adopt a stretch goal: the district would become a 90/90 district with at least 90 percent of its students proficient in both reading and math. In order to achieve that goal, Rafferty maintained a relentless focus on developing the capacity of educators throughout the district to function as members of a PLC. The percentage of students achieving proficiency on the state assessment rose steadily from 76 percent in reading and 80 percent in mathematics in 2005 to 90 percent in reading and 94 percent in math by 2010. The improvement meant 2,100 more of the district's students were able to demonstrate proficiency in 2010 than five years earlier. When the board set its 90/90 goal in 2006, none of Schaumburg's schools had ever achieved that status. By 2010, sixteen had met the goal, and Rafferty was named superintendent of the year in Illinois.

When Anthony Muhammad was named principal of Levey Middle School near Detroit, Michigan, some in the community attributed the dismal performance of the school's students to the fact that they were predominantly poor and African American. Muhammad rejected that premise and was driven by the conviction that the students in his middle school were entitled to the same high-quality education being offered in the best schools in America. Within three years, the number of students failing one or more classes dropped from 150 to 6. Within that same three-year period, the percentage of Levey students demonstrating proficiency on the state test rose from 30 percent to 88 percent in reading and from 31 percent to 78 percent in math—far exceeding the state averages. Muhammad was named Principal of the Year by the Michigan Principal's Association.

Seventy-eight percent of the students who attend Stultz Road Elementary School near Dallas, Texas, are classified as economically disadvantaged and 95 percent are minority. Yet principal Darwin Spiller and his staff adopted a model of "Whatever It Takes" to ensure the academic success of every student. Their commitment to each student led to steadily higher student achievement with more than 95 percent of students demonstrating proficiency in every subject on the Texas Assessment of Knowledge and Skills. The school eliminated achievement gaps between groups of students and increased the percentage of students performing at the commended level on the state assessment by 350 percent over a five-year period. Stultz Road has earned exemplary status from the state for three consecutive years and was one of two schools in Texas to receive the National Distinguished Title I School award in 2011.

Dan Larsen and Andy Conneen are two of the teachers who helped craft the vision statement for the social studies department of Adlai Stevenson High School in suburban Chicago. According to that statement, the discipline of social studies is critical to "democratic values and positive and productive citizenship." The task of social studies teachers is to "give birth again to the American dream—in each new generation, and in each new child." Larsen and Conneen took the commitment to each child very seriously and concluded that a curriculum that reserved honors courses for a select few did not match their democratic principles or the pledge to help every student acquire the knowledge to fulfill his or her responsibilities as a citizen. So they became advocates for opening their advanced placement (AP) American government course to all interested students. They scheduled study sessions in the evenings and weekends to help students meet the requirements of the course. When some students had difficulty attending the study sessions, Larsen and Conneen took to the airwaves and began hosting review sessions over the radio as students called in with their questions. Their radio program was picked up by C-SPAN, which broadcasts it across the nation each year to help students prepare for the AP exam in American government. Larsen and Conneen also maintain a blog on Chicago's CBS news website where they comment on political issues and offer support for students studying government. Their success has encouraged other departments in their school to make their most challenging curriculum accessible to all students, and a school that once had only 7 percent of its graduating class writing AP exams now has over 80 percent writing those exams.

These leaders were driven not only by their belief in the moral imperative of their work, but also by genuine affection for the people they served through that work. They demonstrated what Fullan (2008) has called the first secret of leadership: love those you are attempting to lead. These leaders gush with enthusiasm when describing their staff and their students. They view those with whom they work as the solution to the challenges they face and not the cause of those challenges, and they demonstrate their regard for and commitment to others by creating the conditions to help them succeed.

The superintendent who looks upon building-level leaders with contempt, the principal who demeans the motivation and abilities of the staff, or the teacher who demonstrates disdain for students will be unable to lead effectively. Ultimately, leadership is about love.

To become the best leader you can be, you must fall in love with leading, with the purpose you serve, and the people with whom you work in fulfilling that purpose.

Moral Purpose: Necessary, but Not Sufficient

Although a strong sense of moral imperative is characteristic of great leaders, it is not sufficient to lead effectively. Schools and districts are filled with educators who entered the profession with a sincere desire to make a difference in the lives of students, only to be overwhelmed by the task. The best leaders recognize that leadership requires more than noble intentions; it demands determined doing and an action orientation. The best leaders do not let visionary thinking, planning, and lofty rhetoric substitute for purposeful action. They engage others in clarifying the very specific steps that must be taken to realize the moral purpose they serve.

Effective leaders couple this bias for action with a personal commitment to acquire the knowledge and skills they need to be effective. Whereas ineffective leaders see themselves as already *knowing* everything they need to know, effective leaders see themselves as constantly *learning* about how to get better (Collins, 2009). This learning is not separate from their work—it is deeply embedded within it. They recognize that the deepest learning occurs from taking action, from learning by doing (Lehrer, 2009; Pfeffer & Sutton, 2000). Great leaders are great learners.

To become the best leader you can be, think of learning as the "master skill of leadership" (Kouzes & Posner, 2010, p. 121), never stop learning about how to become more effective, and translate your learning into action.

Leading by Example

The attitudes and actions of district, school, and classroom leaders shape the climate of their respective domains because "the leader's mood is quite literally contagious, spreading quickly and inexorably throughout the organization" (Goleman, Boyatzis, & McKee, 2001). All leaders will confront conditions over which they have no control, but what they can control is how they respond to those situations.

Rather than citing problems in the external environment that others need to solve, effective leaders focus their attention on factors within their own sphere of influence and hold themselves accountable for shaping the outcome through their actions.

Leadership isn't about rank—it's about responsibility. Effective leaders embrace their responsibility for results because they recognize that "the taking of responsibility is the very heart of leadership" (Gardner, 1993, p. 152).

This willingness to be personally accountable for results reflects one of the defining emotions of effective leaders—the belief in their ability to achieve their goals through their efforts. Their optimism does not come from ignoring problems; rather, it comes from the assumption that they have the resources and resolve to solve the problems. As a result, they demonstrate the confidence, resilience, and tenacity to persist in their efforts long after fatalists and pessimists have resigned themselves to their fate.

The link between efficacy and effectiveness has been established for district leaders (Louis et al., 2010), for principals (Marzano et al., 2005; Saphier, 2005), and for teachers (Gallimore et al., 2009; Goddard, Hoy, & Hoy, 2000; Hattie, 2009). Through their actions and words, effective leaders convey their conviction in their personal efficacy and the collective efficacy of those they lead.

When Steve Pearce was named the principal of Jane Addams Junior High School in suburban Chicago, it was the lowest performing of the district's five junior high schools. Some staff members were convinced the school's achievement could not equal some of the other schools in the district because those schools served students of higher socioeconomic status. Pearce, who had successfully led the PLC process at another school prior to coming to Addams, attacked that assumption directly. He expressed his confidence that the staff could help all students learn, and he punctuated that confidence by adopting a new school motto: "No Excuses, No Limits."

Then he took steps to make the motto a reality. He worked with staff to establish more consistent expectations for student behavior. When he discovered that the primary cause of the school's high failure rate was students not completing their homework, he established a program that required them to do so. The school established systematic interventions to provide struggling students with additional time and support for learning. Students who were unable to demonstrate proficiency were required to keep working and learning and then were reassessed upon completion of their intervention. New grading and reporting practices notified parents and counselors of student progress every three weeks. Teachers worked in collaborative teams and used the results of the common assessments they created to improve their practice.

In the first trimester, the number of failing students went from fifty-seven students in the year prior to Pearce's arrival to two students. Skeptical teachers expressed the concern that the change represented grade inflation rather than improvement in student learning. When the state test results came out at the end of the year, however, even the skeptics had to take notice. Students established new achievement records for the school in every subject area and went from worst in the district in reading and math to first in reading and second in mathematics. When the overall achievement of Addams students on the state assessment climbed even higher the next year, the entire staff had compelling evidence that their collective efforts were impacting student learning in a positive way.

Not everyone in an organization must believe it is possible to help students learn at higher levels, but someone must believe in that possibility if that improvement is to occur. That someone must be the leader.

To become the best leader you can be, demonstrate your confidence in the possibility of improvement through the collective efforts of those you lead by putting a process in motion to foster the necessary changes. Then begin to present concrete evidence that improvement is taking place. Celebrate the progress. It is difficult for doubters to remain skeptical when confronted with concrete evidence of irrefutably better results.

Effective Leaders Articulate a Clear, Compelling, and Focused Vision and Connect It to Others' Hopes and Dreams

Peter Drucker (1996) defined a leader as "someone with followers. Without followers there can be no leader" (p. xii). Thus, leadership is as "simple and as complex" as establishing a clear direction for people throughout the organization and influencing them to move in that direction (Louis et al., 2010, p. 6). Anyone can write a vision statement describing a better future for the organization, but it requires effective leadership to create a *shared* vision that addresses the hopes and dreams of people within the organization. Developing shared vision requires dialogue, not monologue, and conversations, not presentations. Shared vision requires leaders who position themselves among those they serve rather than above them.

When Becky Burnette was named the principal of Boones Mill Elementary School in Franklin County, Virginia, she set aside time prior to the school year to meet with every member of the staff in small groups. During these meetings, she asked each small group to react to three questions:

1. What makes this a good school?

2. What is important for me as principal to understand about this school?

3. What could we do to make it an even better school?

She did far more listening than talking, took copious notes, and asked staff members to clarify or expand on their comments.

The one constant that emerged from the dialogue was the universal desire for more *time*—time to teach, time to intervene for students who struggled, time to meet with colleagues, and time to plan. So Becky met with teacher leaders to create a schedule and to develop a plan to provide staff with the one thing that was clearly most precious to them—the gift of time. The teacher leaders then worked with staff to build shared knowledge about how they could use that time to engage in the work of a PLC (although they never used the term). The staff agreed that this was what they wanted for their school, and they established a shared vision of a new Boones Mill Elementary. Within three years, Boones Mill became one of the first elementary schools in Virginia to win the United States Department of Education's NCLB Blue Ribbon Award.

Notice that Becky did not say to her staff, "I am your leader. Listen to me as I articulate my personal vision for this school." Instead she was able to say, "I have listened to you and your colleagues, and I have some ideas for helping us realize your aspirations for our school." Like all great leaders, she was able to establish a common cause and become the steward of a widely shared vision.

The ability to articulate a realistic, credible, attractive vision of the future that connects to the hopes and dreams of others is a defining skill of an effective leader. When thousands of people were asked to describe what they want in a leader, their answers were very similar to their response regarding what they look for in a colleague: honesty, competence, intelligence, supportiveness, and so on. The only striking difference in the responses came in one area: forward thinking. People want leaders who are thinking ahead and helping define a better future (Kouzes & Posner, 2010).

In order for a shared vision to impact the day-to-day work of people throughout an organization, its members must be able to understand how their work contributes to a larger purpose. So effective leaders constantly remind people of the significance of their work and how it is contributing to an important collective endeavor (Katzenbach & Kahn, 2010). One of the most important motivators in any organization is the belief that the work being done is valuable and worthwhile, that it is making a positive difference in the world. Effective leaders give the "gift of significance" (Bolman & Deal, 2001, p. 95) by helping people throughout the organization find meaning in their work by linking it to a higher purpose and celebrating its importance (Amabile & Kramer, 2010).

Mount Eagle Elementary School in Fairfax County, Virginia, has 77 percent of its students living in poverty compared to a state average of 33 percent. Ninety-five percent of those students are minority compared to a state average of 33 percent. Yet in 2010, Mount Eagle students outperformed the state's student achievement in every subject area of Virginia's assessment. Ninety percent or more of the students demonstrated proficiency in each subject area.

When the staff returned for the start of a new school year, Principal Brian Butler led the celebration of this tangible evidence that their sustained focus on improving student learning had generated such outstanding results. He then showed a video with the smiling faces of individual students, one after another, while the song "How to Save a Life" played. At its conclusion, he advised the staff that each of the students in the video had been unable to demonstrate proficiency on one or more parts of the state assessment. He reminded them of the strong correlation between student achievement in elementary school and ultimate success or failure in high school. He offered chilling statistics describing the predictable future of high school dropouts. He asked the staff to recognize that for many of their students, Mount Eagle was their last best hope for having access to the American dream. Finally, he called upon them to recommit to the school's mission of ensuring success for *each* student, and solicited their ideas for how they could intervene for students who were not being successful. Brian used data to celebrate improvement at the same time he touched the hearts of staff members by reminding them of the importance of each individual student. He helped everyone on the staff recognize the significance of their work.

To be the best leader you can be, link the vision of your district, school, or classroom to the hopes and dreams of those you serve. Work with a guiding coalition to develop the specific actionable steps you will take to move toward the vision. Then constantly remind your staff or students of the importance of their work by linking it to a higher purpose.

Effective Leaders Help Those They Lead Feel More Capable by Helping Them Become More Capable

Think of the best leader you have ever known, the leader you most admire, and describe your relationship with that person. James Kouzes and Barry Posner (2010) have asked this question over three decades to thousands of people and report the following:

> People said the leader made them feel empowered, listened to, understood, capable, important, like they mattered, challenged to do more. The overwhelming sense we get from thousands and thousands of these responses is that the best leaders take action that make people feel strong and capable. They make people feel they can do more than they thought they could. (p. 69)

People did not report a sense of awe because of the leader's personal brilliance. They did not feel a sense of inadequacy by being in the presence of someone determined to demonstrate he or she was the smartest person in the room. They felt empowered because the leader was committed to helping them be successful in their work.

As we have stressed throughout this book, effective empowerment does not mean encouraging people to go off and do whatever they want. It means creating the conditions that help people succeed. Those conditions include:

- Establishing clear purpose, priorities, and parameters that allow people to be creative and autonomous within clearly established boundaries

- Providing people with access to the resources that enable them to make informed decisions rather than pooling opinions

- Engaging them in establishing clear, unambiguous benchmarks so they can monitor their own progress

- Ensuring they have relevant and timely data that informs their practice and allows them to make adjustments

- Building the capacity of people to be successful in what they are attempting to do by providing them with training, support, and resources that lead to their success

Finally, empowerment means establishing a culture in which people are hungry for evidence and are willing to face the brutal facts when things don't work out as hoped. Evidence must be used to inform and improve rather than demean and punish (Collins, 2009). In the right culture, transparency about practice and results is viewed as a vital tool for continuous improvement (Fullan, 2010b; Katzenbach & Kahn, 2010). In the wrong culture, people view benchmarks, data, and results as proof that they are monitored too closely, are not trusted, or are about to be punished (Kanter, 2004).

Whittier Union High School District, located ten miles from central Los Angeles, serves ten thousand students in its five comprehensive high schools and one continuation school. In 2004, Superintendent Sandy Thorstenson began laying the groundwork for improving student achievement by having principals and teacher leaders read books on the PLC process and accompanying them on a series of field trips to a nationally recognized high school that had a long history of success as a PLC. She then engaged them in dialogue, solicited their perspectives, and answered their questions. Once she felt that the district had met its obligation to build shared knowledge, she stipulated three conditions she expected to see in all of the district's schools:

1. Every school would implement common assessments created at both the district and site levels.

2. Every school would provide and protect time for teacher collaboration.

3. Every school would implement academic interventions within the daily schedule (Cox, 2008).

Each school had discretion to determine how it would address these priorities, but while the details of implementation could vary from school to school, the intended outcomes could not. Thorstenson established three measurable indicators to monitor each school's success in helping more students achieve at higher levels.

Thorstenson then began to identify and develop leaders throughout the district to help meet the challenge she had presented. She conducted weekly principal meetings to support principals in identifying and overcoming obstacles. She created the position of lead teacher and appointed 123 teachers from within the district to that role to assume responsibility for leading the implementation of the common assessment process. She assigned one person in each school to help teachers organize and retrieve the data they needed to identify the strengths and weaknesses in student learning. Other people within the schools were named intervention specialists and given a released period to coordinate the school plan of intervention for students who struggled. The district redefined the role of guidance counselor to give counselors key leadership responsibilities for creating the specific steps and strategies that constituted the system of intervention in their schools. The teacher union played a critical leadership role in the entire improvement process, and many union leaders served as lead teachers and intervention specialists.

The focus on and transparency of results from common assessments made it possible for individual teacher leaders to emerge from within the ranks and to impact practice throughout the district. A teacher whose students achieved at extraordinarily high levels could train not only the colleagues on his team, but also teachers throughout the district on the strategies leading to those results.

Thorstenson's strategy of empowerment meant that hundreds of Whittier educators assumed new leadership roles. As a result, the district has experienced dramatic gains in student achievement across all measures and in every one of its schools. A study conducted by researchers from the University of Southern California lauded Whittier for being one of the few districts in the state in which *every* school was outperforming similar schools. The researchers attributed Whittier's success to "the District's unwavering 'laser-like' focus on implementing its 'Whatever It Takes' initiative and its tremendous leadership at all levels—from the Board and Superintendent to teachers" (Whittier Union High School District, 2008, p. 1). The researchers applauded Whittier for creating "a culture of success." This success has occurred even though the district's budget has been slashed due to the ongoing financial crisis in California and despite the fact that the percentage of Whittier students living in poverty has increased from 28 percent in 2002 to over 70 percent in 2010.

The remarkable success of Whittier Union did not occur by giving license to each school to pursue its own objective or providing unfettered autonomy to each staff member to focus on his or her unique interests. Whittier educators were very clear about their priorities, and they were held accountable. At the same time, however, they were also empowered to be very creative within the framework of those priorities.

We do not offer these stories of remarkable leaders to convince you that the key to improving schools is to find heroic individuals. Schools have always had heroic individuals who go far beyond the call of duty. The key to leadership is developing the capacity of others to accomplish a collective endeavor, not doing it all yourself. As Thomas Sergiovanni (2005) wrote, "Leaders minister to the needs of the school by being of service and providing help. The test of moral leadership is whether the competence, well-being, and independence of the follower is enhanced . . . and whether the enterprise of which both are a part ultimately benefits" (p. 19).

To be the best leader you can be, don't hoard power; give it away. Don't view yourself as the heroic individual who will single-handedly improve your district, school, or classroom; view yourself as a hero-maker who develops the leadership potential of those you serve. You will know you have succeeded when you realize that you could leave and the organization will continue to improve because of the many leaders that remain.

Conclusion

Every superintendent, principal, and teacher is in a leadership position. Don't ask if you are leading. You are. Don't ask if you will make a difference. You will. The question is, "What kind of leader will you be, and what kind of difference you will make?" Will you approach your work as a calling or a job? Will you love those you serve or demean them? Will you translate your convictions into purposeful action and challenging goals or settle for the nobleness of your good intentions? Will you continue to learn how to be more effective, or will you be satisfied that you know enough? Will you focus on what is within your sphere of influence and dedicate yourself to making it better, or will you assign both blame for your current reality and responsibility for improving it to others? Will you demonstrate a passionate conviction that by working collaboratively you can accomplish great things, or will you succumb to fatalism and cynicism? Will you link your efforts to the hopes and dreams of those you serve, or will you pursue your own agenda? Will you seek evidence of effectiveness to fuel continuous improvement or to punish? Will you constantly remind those you hope to influence of the significance of the work they do and challenge them to do it well, or will you settle for mediocrity?

Robert Greenleaf (1970) differentiated between what he called "leader-first leaders" and "servant-first leaders." The leader-first leader seeks leadership for personal power and gain. The servant-first leader "begins with the natural feeling that one wants to serve . . . to make sure that others' highest priorities are met. The best test, and the most difficult to administer is: Do they grow as persons? Do they, *while being served*, become healthier, wiser, freer, more autonomous, more likely themselves to become servants?" (p. 7).

May you choose to be a servant leader, and in making that choice, may you develop the capacity of those you serve to carry on your legacy by becoming servant leaders themselves.

References and Resources

Ainsworth, L., & Viegut, D. (2006). *Common formative assessments.* Thousand Oaks, CA: Corwin Press.

Alliance for Excellent Education. (2008). *Dropouts, diplomas, and dollars: U.S. high schools and the nation's economy.* Washington, DC: Author. Accessed at www.all4ed.org/files/Econ2008.pdf on January 21, 2011.

Amabile, T., & Kramer, S. (2010). What really motivates workers: Understanding the power of progress. *Harvard Business Review, 88*(1), 44–45.

Anderson, J. R., Reder, L. M., & Simon, H. A. (1995). *Applications and misapplications of cognitive psychology to mathematics education.* Unpublished manuscript, Carnegie Mellon University. Accessed at http://act.psy.cmu.edu/personal/ja/misapplied.html on January 21, 2011.

Anderson, L. W., Krathwohl, D. R., Airasian, P. W., Cruikshank, K. A., Mayer, R. E., Pintrich, P. R. et al. (Eds.). (2001). *A taxonomy for learning, teaching, and assessing: A revision of Bloom's taxonomy of educational objectives.* New York: Longman.

Annenberg Institute for School Reform. (2005). *Professional learning communities: Professional development strategies that improve instruction.* Providence, RI: Author. Accessed at www.annenberginstitute.org/pdf/ProfLearning.pdf on January 18, 2010.

Barber, M., & Mourshed, M. (2007). *How the world's best-performing school systems come out on top.* New York: McKinsey & Company. Accessed at www.mckinsey.com/App_Media/Reports/SSO/Worlds_School_Systems_Final.pdf on January 1, 2010.

Barber, M., & Mourshed, M. (2009). *Shaping the future: How good education systems can become great in the decade ahead—Report on the International Education Roundtable.* New York: McKinsey & Company. Accessed at www.mckinsey.com/locations/southeastasia /knowledge/Education_ Roundtable.pdf on December 20, 2010.

Barth, R. (1990). *Improving schools from within: Teachers, parents, and principals can make the difference.* San Francisco: Jossey-Bass.

Black, P., & Wiliam, D. (1998a). Assessment and classroom learning. *Assessment in Education, 5*(1), 7–75.

Black, P., & Wiliam, D. (1998b). Inside the black box: Raising standards through classroom assessment. *Phi Delta Kappan, 80*(2), 139–148. Accessed at www.pdkintl.org/kappan/kbla9810.htm on May 5, 2009.

Blanchard, K. (2007). *Leading at a higher level: Blanchard on leadership and creating high performing organizations.* Upper Saddle River, NJ: Prentice Hall.

Bolman, L. G., & Deal, T. E. (2001). *Leading with soul: An uncommon journey of spirit.* San Francisco: Jossey-Bass.

Brooks, D. (2005, October 6). Pillars of cultural capital. *New York Times.* www.leadertoleader.org/knowledgecenter/journal.aspx?ArticleID=50

Bruner, J. S. (1973). *Beyond the information given.* New York: W.W. Norton.

Bryk, A., & Schneider, B. (2004). *Trust in schools: A core resource for improvement.* New York: Russell Sage.

Buckingham, M. (2005). *The one thing you need to know . . . about great managing, great leading and sustained individual success.* New York: Free Press.

Buddin, R., & Zamarro, G. (2009). *Teacher qualifications and student achievement in urban elementary schools.* Santa Monica, CA: RAND. Accessed at www.rand.org/pubs/reprints/2010/RAND_RP1410.pdf on July 1, 2010.

Buffum, A., Mattos, M., & Weber, C. (2010). The why behind RTI. *Educational Leadership, 68*(2), 10–16.

Buffum, A., Mattos, M., & Weber, C. (in press). *The four C's of RTI: Rethinking and simplifying RTI.* Bloomington, IN: Solution Tree Press.

Bureau of Labor Statistics. (2009). *Economic news release: Employment projections—2008-2018 summary.* Washington, DC: Author. Accessed at www.bls.gov/news.release/ecopro.nro.htm on January 21, 2011.

Bush, G. H. W. (1989, October 1). 'A Jeffersonian compact'; The statement by the president and governors. *New York Times*. Accessed at http://query.nytimes.com/gst/fullpage.html?res=950DE7DB1330F932A3575 3C1A96F948260 on January 21, 2011.

Bushaw, W., & McNee, J. (2009). Americans speak out: The 41st annual Phi Delta Kappa/Gallup Poll of the public's attitudes toward public schools. *Phi Delta Kappan, 91*(1), 9–23.

Carpenter, W. (2000). Ten years of silver bullets: Dissenting thoughts on education reform. *Phi Delta Kappan, 81*(5), 383–389.

Carroll, T. (2009). The next generation of learning teams. *Phi Delta Kappan, 91*(2), 8–13.

Carroll, T., Fulton, K., & Doerr, H. (2010). *Team up for 21st century teaching and learning: What research and practice reveal about professional learning*. Washington, DC: National Commission on Teaching and America's Future.

Catrambone, R. (1998). The subgoal learning model: Creating better examples so that students can solve novel problems. *Journal of Experimental Psychology: General, 127*, 355–376.

Center for Research on Education Outcomes. (2009). *Multiple choice: Charter school performance in 16 states—Executive summary*. Stanford, CA: Author. Accessed at http://credo.stanford.edu/reports/MULTIPLE_CHOICE_EXECUTIVE%20SUMSUMM.pdf on January 21, 2011.

Cepeda, N. J., Pashler, H., Vul, E., Wixted, J. T., & Rohrer, D. (2006). Distributed practice in verbal recall tasks: A review and quantitative synthesis. *Psychological Bulletin, 132*, 354–380.

Chenoweth, K. (2009). It can be done, it's being done, and here's how. *Phi Delta Kappan, 91*(1), 38–43.

City, E. A., Elmore, R. F., Fiarman, S. E., & Teitel, L. (2009). *Instructional rounds in education: A network approach to improving teaching and learning*. Cambridge, MA: Harvard University Press.

College Board. (2010). *The 6th annual AP Report to the Nation*. New York: College Board. Accessed at www.collegeboard.com/html/aprtn/highlights.html on January 21, 2011.

Collins, J. (2009). *How the mighty fall: And why some companies never give in*. New York: HarperCollins.

Common Core State Standards Initiative. (2010). *Common core state standards for English language arts & literacy in history/social studies, science, and technical subjects.* Washington, DC: National Governors Association Center for Best Practices and the Council of Chief State School Officers.

Conzemius, A., & O'Neill, J. (2002). *The handbook for SMART school teams.* Bloomington, IN: Solution Tree Press.

Cooper, G., & Sweller, J. (1987). The effects of schema acquisition and rule automation on mathematical problem-solving transfer. *Journal of Educational Psychology, 79,* 347–362.

Cox, K. B. (2008). What's working in Whittier. *Educational Leadership, 65*(8). Accessed at www.ascd.org/publications/educational_leadership/may08/vol65/num08/What's_Working_in_Whittier.aspx on January 21, 2011.

Darling-Hammond, L. (2010). *The flat world and education: How America's commitment to equity will determine our future.* New York: Teachers College Press.

Desimone, L., Porter, A., Garet, M., Yoon, K., & Birman, B. (2002). Effects of professional development on teachers' instruction: Results from a three-year longitudinal study. *Educational Evaluation and Policy Analysis, 24*(2), 81–112.

Dolejs, C. (2006). *Report on key practices and policies of consistently higher performing high schools.* Washington, DC: National High School Center. Accessed at www.betterhighschools.org/docs/ReportOfKeyPracticesandPolicies_10–31–06.pdf on January 10, 2010.

Drucker, P. (1992). *Managing for the future: The 1990s and beyond.* New York: Truman Talley Books.

Drucker, P. (1996). Not enough generals were killed. In F. Hesselbein, M. Goldsmith, & R. Beckhard (Eds.), *The leader of the future: New visions, strategies and practices for the next era* (pp. xi–xvi). San Francisco: Jossey-Bass.

Duffett, A., Farkas, S., Rotherham, A. J., & Silva, E. (2008). *Waiting to be won over: Teachers speak on the profession, unions, and reform.* Washington, DC: Education Sector.

DuFour, R., DuFour, R., & Eaker, R. (2008). *Revisiting professional learning communities at work: New insights for improving schools.* Bloomington, IN: Solution Tree Press.

DuFour, R., DuFour, R., Eaker, R., & Karhanek, G. (2010). *Raising the bar and closing the gap: Whatever it takes.* Bloomington, IN: Solution Tree Press.

DuFour, R., DuFour, R., Eaker, R., & Many, T. (2010). *Learning by doing: A handbook for professional learning communities at work.* (2nd ed.). Bloomington, IN: Solution Tree Press.

DuFour, R., & Marzano, R. (2009). How teachers learn: High-leverage strategies for principal leadership. *Educational Leadership, 66*(5), 62–68.

Duschl, R. A., Schweingruber, H. A., & Shouse, A. W. (2007). *Taking science to school: Learning and teaching science in grades K–8.* Washington, DC: National Research Council.

Dweck, C. (2006). *Mindset: The new psychology of success.* New York: Ballantine Books.

Elmore, R. (2003). *School reform from the inside out: Policy, practice, and performance.* Boston: Harvard Education Press.

Evans, R. (2001). *The human side of school change: Reform, resistance and the real-life problems of innovation.* San Francisco: Jossey-Bass.

Farr, S. (2010). Leadership, not magic. *Educational Leadership, 68*(4), 28–33.

Fiske, E. (1992). *Smart schools, smart kids: Why do some schools work?* New York: Simon & Schuster.

Fullan, M. (1997). Emotion and hope: Constructive concepts for complex times. In A. Hargreaves (Ed.), *Rethinking educational change with heart and mind* (pp. 216–232). Alexandria, VA: Association for Supervision and Curriculum Development.

Fullan, M. (2007). *The new meaning of educational change* (4th ed.). New York: Teachers College Press.

Fullan, M. (2008). *The six secrets of change: What the best organizations do to help their organizations survive and thrive.* San Francisco: Jossey-Bass.

Fullan, M. (2010a). *All systems go.* Thousand Oaks, CA: Corwin Press.

Fullan, M. (2010b). *The moral imperative realized.* Thousand Oaks, CA: Corwin Press.

Fullan, M. (2010c). *Motion leadership: The skinny on becoming change savvy.* Thousand Oaks, CA: Corwin Press.

Fulton, K., Yoon, I., & Lee, C. (2005). *Induction into learning communities.* Washington, DC: National Commission on Teaching and America's Future.

Gallimore, R., Ermeling, B., Saunders, W., & Goldenberg, C. (2009). Moving the learning of teaching closer to practice: Teacher education implications of school-based inquiry teams. *Elementary School Journal, 109*(5), 537–551.

Gardner, J. (1993). *On leadership.* New York: Free Press.

Garmston, R., & Wellman, B. (1999). *The adaptive school: A sourcebook for developing collaborative groups.* Norwood, MA: Christopher-Gordon.

Goddard, R. D., Hoy, W. K., & Hoy, A. W. (2000). Collective teacher efficacy: Its meaning, measure, and impact on student achievement. *American Educational Research Journal, 37*(2), 479–507.

Goddard, R. D., Hoy, W. K., & Hoy, A. W. (2004). Collective efficacy beliefs: Theoretical developments, empirical evidence, and future directions. *Educational Researcher, 33*(3), 3–13.

Goleman, D., Boyatzis, R., & McKee, A. (2001). Primal leadership: The hidden driver of great performance. *Harvard Business Review.* Accessed at http://hbr.org/2001/12/primal-leadership/ar/1 on January 21, 2011.

Goleman, D., Boyatzis, R., & McKee, A. (2002). *Primal leadership: Learning to lead with emotional intelligence.* Boston: Harvard Business School Press.

Goodlad, J. (1984). *A place called school: Prospects for the future.* New York: McGraw-Hill.

Greenleaf, R. (1970). *The servant as leader.* Indianapolis, IN: Robert K. Greenleaf Center for Servant-Leadership.

Hanushek, E., & Rivkin, S. (2006). Teacher quality. In E. Hanushek & F. Welch (Eds.), *Handbook of the economics of education* (Vol. 2, pp. 1051–1078). Amsterdam: Elsevier. Accessed at http://edpro.stanford .edu/hanushek/admin/pages/files/uploads/HESEDU2018.pdf on July 1, 2010.

Hargreaves, A. (2004). Broader purpose calls for higher understanding: An interview with Andy Hargreaves. *Journal of Staff Development, 25*(2), 46–50.

Harvard Graduate School of Education. (2008). Study finds Teach for America teachers stay in the classroom past initial commitment [Press release]. Accessed at www.gse.harvard.edu/news_events /features/2008/05/21_project.php on January 21, 2011.

Hattie, J. (1984). An empirical study of various indices for determining unidimensionality. *Multivariate Behavioral Research, 19*, 49–78.

Hattie, J. (1985). Methodology review: Assessing the unidimensionality of tests and items. *Applied Psychological Measurement, 9*(2), 139–164.

Hattie, J. (2009). *Visible learning: A synthesis of over 800 meta-analyses relating to student achievement.* New York: Routledge.

Hattie, J., Krakowksi, K., Rogers, H. J., & Swaminthan, H. (1996). An assessment of Stout's index of essential unidimensionality. *Applied Psychological Measurement, 20*(1), 1–14.

Haycock, K. (1998). Good teaching matters . . . a lot. *Thinking K–16, 3*(2), 1–14.

Herman, J. L., & Choi, K. (2008). *Formative assessment and the improvement of middle science learning: The role of teacher advocacy* (CRESST Report 740). Los Angeles: National Center for Research on Evaluation, Standards, and Student Testing.

Hernez-Broome, G., & Hughes, R. (2004). Leadership development: Past, present, and future. *Human Resource Planning, 27*(1), 24–32.

Hirsch, E. D., Jr. (1996). *The schools we need and why we don't have them.* New York: Doubleday.

Husen, T. (Ed.). (1967). *International study of achievement in mathematics* (Vol. 2). New York: Wiley.

Inskeep, S. (2010, March 2). Former No Child Left Behind advocate turns critic. *Morning Edition.* Accessed at www.npr.org/templates/story /story.php?storyId=124209100 on January 21, 2011.

Institute of Education Sciences, & National Center for Education Research. (2007). *Organizing instruction and study to improve student learning.* Washington, DC: Author.

International Reading Association Commission on RTI. (2009). Working draft of guiding principles. *Reading Today, 26*(4), 1, 4–6.

Jalongo, M. R., Rieg, S. A., & Helterbran, V. R. (2007). *Planning for learning: Collaborative approaches to lesson design and review.* New York: Teachers College Press.

Joyce, B., & Weil, M. (1986). *Models of teaching* (3rd ed.). Englewood Cliffs, NJ: Prentice Hall.

Kanter, R. M. (1999). The enduring skills of change leaders. *Leader to Leader, 13,* 15–22. Accessed at www.leadertoleader.org/knowledge-center/journal.aspx?ArticleID=50 on January 10, 2010.

Kanter, R. M. (2004). *Confidence: How winning streaks and losing streaks begin and end.* New York: Three Rivers Press.

Katzenbach, J., & Kahn, Z. (2010). *Leading outside the lines: How to mobilize the (in)formal organization, energize your team, and get better results.* San Francisco: Jossey-Bass.

Katzenbach, J. R., & Smith, D. K. (2003). *The wisdom of teams: Creating the high-performance organization.* Boston: Harvard Business School Press.

Kegan, R., & Lahey, L. (2001). *How the way we talk can change the way we work: Seven languages for transformation.* San Francisco: Jossey-Bass.

Kolata, G. (2007, January 3). A surprising secret to a long life: Stay in school. *New York Times.* Accessed at www.nytimes.com/2007/01/03/health/03aging.html?ex=1325480400&en=b8ffe66abf1b1466&ei=5088&partner=rssnyt&emc=rss on January 21, 2011.

Korbin, J., Sathy, V., & Shaw, E. (2007). *A historical view of subgroup performance differences on the SAT Reasoning Test* (College Board Research Report No. 2006-5). New York: College Board. Accessed at http://professionals.collegeboard.com/profdownload/pdf/06-1868%20RDCBR06-5_070105.pdf on May 31, 2010.

Kotter, J. P. (1996). *Leading change.* Boston: Harvard Business School Press.

Kouzes, J., & Posner, B. (1987). *The leadership challenge: How to get extraordinary things done in organizations.* San Francisco: Jossey-Bass.

Kouzes, J., & Posner, B. (2003). Challenge is the opportunity for greatness. *Leader to Leader, 28,* 16–23.

Kouzes, J., & Posner, B. (2010). *The truth about leadership: The no-fads, heart-of-the-matter facts you need to know.* San Francisco: Jossey-Bass.

Krathwohl, D. R., & Payne, D. A. (1971). Defining and assessing educational objectives. In R. L. Thorndike (Ed.), *Educational measurement* (pp. 17–45). Washington, DC: American Council on Education.

Kruse, S., Seashore Louis, K., & Bryk, A. (1995). *Building professional learning community in schools.* Madison, WI: Center for School Organization and Restructuring.

Lehrer, J. (2009). *How we decide.* Boston: Houghton Mifflin Harcourt.

Leithwood, K., Seashore Louis, K., Anderson, S., & Wahlstrom, K. (2004). *How leadership influences student learning.* New York: Wallace Foundation.

Lencioni, P. (2003). The trouble with teamwork. *Leader to Leader, 29,* 35–40.

Lencioni, P. (2005). *Overcoming the five dysfunctions of a team: A field guide for leaders, managers, and facilitators.* San Francisco: Jossey-Bass.

Lewin, T., & Dillion, S. (2010, April 20). Districts warn of deeper teacher cuts. *New York Times.* Accessed at www.nytimes.com/2010/04/21 /education/21teachers.html on January 21, 2011.

Lezotte, L. W. (2008). *Effective schools: Past, present, and future.* Okemos, MI: Effective Schools Products. Accessed at www.effectiveschools .com/images/stories/brockpaper.pdf on January 21, 2011.

Lieberman, A., & Rosenholtz, S. (1987). The road to school improvement: Barriers and bridges. In J. Goodlad (Ed.), *The ecology of school renewal: Eighty-sixth yearbook of the National Society for the Study of Education* (pp. 79–98). Chicago: National Society for the Study of Education.

Lincoln, A. (1953). Annual message to Congress. In R. P. Basler (Ed.), *The collected works of Abraham Lincoln* (Vol. 5). New Brunswick, NJ: Rutgers University Press.

Linden, R. (2003). The discipline of collaboration. *Leader to Leader, 29,* 41–47. Accessed at www.pfdf.org/knowledgecenter/journal .aspx?ArticleID=81 on July 3, 2010.

Little, J. (2006). *Professional community and professional development in the learning-centered school.* Washington, DC: National Education Association. Accessed at www.nea.org/assets/docs/mf_pdreport.pdf on January 18, 2010.

Louis, K., Leithwood, K., Wahlstrom, K., & Anderson, S. (2010). *Learning from leadership: Investigating the links to improved student achievement.* Minneapolis: University of Minnesota.

Mager, R. F. (1962). *Preparing instructional objectives.* Palo Alto, CA: Fearon.

Markow, D., & Pieters, A. (2010). *The 2009 MetLife survey of the American teacher: Collaborating for student success.* New York: MetLife Foundation. Accessed at www.metlife.com/about/corporate-profile /citizenship/metlife-foundation/metlife-survey-of-the-american -teacher.html?WT.mc_id=vu1101 on January 21, 2011.

Marzano, R. J. (2002). A comparison of selected methods of scoring classroom assessments. *Applied Measurement in Education, 15*(3), 249–268.

Marzano, R. J. (2003). *What works in schools: Translating research into action.* Alexandria, VA: Association for Supervision and Curriculum Development.

Marzano, R. J. (2004). *Building background knowledge for academic achievement.* Alexandria, VA: Association for Supervision and Curriculum Development.

Marzano, R. J. (2006). *Classroom assessment and grading that work.* Alexandria, VA: Association for Supervision and Curriculum Development.

Marzano, R. J. (2007). *The art and science of teaching: A comprehensive framework for effective instruction.* Alexandria, VA: Association for Supervision and Curriculum Development.

Marzano, R. J. (2009a). *Designing and teaching learning goals and objectives.* Bloomington, IN: Marzano Research Laboratory.

Marzano, R. J. (2009b). Setting the record straight on "high-yield" strategies. *Phi Delta Kappan, 91*(1), 30–37.

Marzano, R. J. (2010a). Developing expert teachers. In R. J. Marzano (Ed.), *On excellence in teaching* (pp. 213–246). Bloomington, IN: Solution Tree Press.

Marzano, R. J. (2010b). *Formative assessment and standards-based grading.* Bloomington, IN: Marzano Research Laboratory.

Marzano, R. J., & Brown, J. L. (2009). *A handbook for the art and science of teaching.* Alexandria, VA: Association for Supervision and Curriculum Development.

Marzano, R. J., Frontier, T., & Livingston, D. (in press). *Effective supervision: Supporting the art and science of teaching.* Alexandria, VA: Association for Supervision and Curriculum Development.

Marzano, R. J., & Haystead, M. W. (2008). *Making standards useful in the classroom.* Alexandria, VA: Association for Supervision and Curriculum Development.

Marzano, R. J., & Kendall, J. S. (2007). *The new taxonomy of educational objectives* (2nd ed.). Thousand Oaks, CA: Corwin Press.

Marzano, R. J., & Kendall, J. S. (2008). *Designing and assessing educational objectives: Applying the new taxonomy.* Thousand Oaks, CA: Corwin Press.

Marzano, R. J., Kendall, J. S., & Cicchinelli, L. F. (1998). *What Americans believe students should know: A survey of U.S. adults.* Aurora, CO: Mid-continent Regional Educational Laboratory.

Marzano, R. J., Kendall, J. S., & Gaddy, B. B. (1999). *Essential knowledge: The debate over what American students should know.* Aurora, CO: Mid-continent Regional Educational Laboratory.

Marzano, R. J., & Waters, T. (2009). *District leadership that works: Striking the right balance.* Bloomington, IN: Solution Tree Press.

Marzano, R. J., Waters, T., & McNulty, B. A. (2005). *School leadership that works: From research to results.* Alexandria, VA: Association for Supervision and Curriculum Development.

McCauley, C., & Van Velsor, E. (2003). *The Center for Creative Leadership handbook of leadership development.* San Francisco: Jossey-Bass.

McDougall, D., Saunders, W., & Goldenberg, C. (2007). Inside the black box of school reform: Explaining the how and why of change at getting results in schools. *International Journal of Disability, Development, and Education, 54*(1), 51–89.

McKinsey & Company. (2009). *The economic impact of the achievement gap in America's schools.* New York: Author. Accessed at www.mck

insey.com/App_Media/Images/Page_Images/Offices/SocialSector
/PDF/achievement_gap_report.pdf on January 21, 2011.

McLaughlin, M., & Talbert, J. (2006). *Building school-based teacher
learning communities: Professional strategies to improve student
achievement.* New York: Teachers College Press.

Mourshed, M., Chijioke, C., & Barber, M. (2010). *How the world's most
improved school systems keep getting better.* New York: McKinsey &
Company. Accessed at http://ssomckinsey.darbyfilms.com/reports
/EducationBook_A4%20SINGLES_DDE%202.pdf on January 21, 2011.

National Assessment of Educational Progress. (2007). *The nation's report
card: America's high school graduates—Results from the 2005 high
school transcript study.* Washington, DC: Author. Accessed at http://
nationsreportcard.gov/hsts_2005/hs_over_1.asp on January 21, 2011.

National Association of Secondary School Principals. (1995). *Breaking
ranks: Changing an American institution.* Reston, VA: Author.

National Center for Public Policy and Higher Education. (2005). *Policy
alert: Income of U.S. workforce projected to decline* if *education doesn't
improve.* San Jose, CA: Author. Accessed at www.highereducation
.org/reports/pa_decline/pa_decline.pdf on January 21, 2011.

National Center on Response to Intervention. (2008). *What is RTI?*
[webinar]. Washington, DC: Author. Accessed at www.rti4success
.org/index.php?option=com_content &task=blogcategory&id=22&It
emid=79 on January 21, 2011.

National Commission on Excellence in Education. *A nation at risk.*
Accessed at www.ed.gov/pubs/NatAtRisk/risk.html on January 21,
2011.

National Commission on Teaching and America's Future. (2003). *No
dream denied: A pledge to America's children.* Washington, DC:
Author.

National Education Commission on Time and Learning. (1994).
*Prisoners of time: Report of the National Education Commission on
Time and Learning.* Washington, DC: U.S. Government Printing
Office.

National Governors Association, Council of Chief State School Officers,
& Achieve, Inc. (2008). *Benchmarking for success: Ensuring U.S.
students receive a world-class education.* Washington, DC: National

Governors Association. Accessed at www.corestandards.org /assets/0812BENCHMARKING.pdf on January 21, 2011.

National Staff Development Council. (2001). *Collaboration skills.* Accessed at www.nsdc.org/standards/collaborationskills.cfm on January 21, 2011.

Newmann, F., & Wehlage, G. (1995). *Successful school restructuring: A report to the public and educators by the Center for Restructuring Schools.* Madison: University of Wisconsin.

Newton, A. & Collins, R. (2008). *Petition.* Accessed at www.fivefreedoms .org/5freedoms/petition on January 21, 2011.

Odden, A. R., & Archibald, S. J. (2009). *Doubling student performance . . . and finding the resources to do it.* Thousand Oaks, CA: Corwin Press.

Odden, A., & Wallace, M. (2003). Leveraging teacher pay. *Education Week, 22*(43), 6.

O'Hora, D., & Maglieri, K. (2006). Goal statements and goal-directed behavior: A relational frame account of goal setting in organizations. *Journal of Organizational Behavior Management, 26*(1), 131–170.

Olson, L. (2007, June 26). Harvard project boils down ingredients for district success. *Education Week.* Accessed at www.edweek.org/ew /articles/2007/06/26/43pelp_web.h26.html?qs=harvard+projpro+boils on January 21, 2011.

O'Neil, J. (1995). On schools as learning organizations: A conversation with Peter Senge. *Educational Leadership, 52*(7), 20–23.

O'Neill, J., & Conzemius, A. (2005). *The power of SMART goals: Using goals to improve student learning.* Bloomington, IN: Solution Tree Press.

Organisation for Economic Co-operation and Development. (2009). *Education at a glance 2009: OECD indicators.* Paris: Author.

Organisation for Economic Co-operation and Development. (2010). *Education at a glance 2010: OECD indicators.* Paris: Author.

Patterson, K., Grenny, J., Maxfield, D., McMillan, R., & Switzler, A. (2008). *Influencer: The power to change anything.* New York: McGraw-Hill.

Patterson, K., Grenny, J., McMillan, R., & Switzler, A. (2002). *Crucial conversations: Tools for talking when stakes are high.* New York: McGraw-Hill.

Petrelli, M. (2007). Is No Child Left Behind's birthday worth celebrating? *Education Gadfly, 7*(1). Accessed at www.fordhamfoundation .org/foundation/gadfly/issue.cfm?edition=&id=271#3173 on May 20, 2010.

Pfeffer, J., & Sutton, R. (2000). *The knowing-doing gap: How smart companies turn knowledge into action.* Boston: Harvard Business School Press.

Pfeffer, J., & Sutton, R. (2006). *Hard facts, dangerous half-truths and total nonsense: Profiting from evidence-based management.* Boston: Harvard Business School Press.

Popham, W. J. (2009a). Curriculum mistakes to avoid. *American School Board Journal, 196*(11), 36–38.

Popham, W. J. (2009b). *Unlearned lessons: Six stumbling blocks to our schools' success.* Cambridge, MA: Harvard Education Press.

President's Commission on Excellence in Special Education. (2002). *A new era: Revitalizing special education for children and their families.* Washington, DC: U.S. Department of Education, President's Commission on Excellence in Special Education, Office of Special Education and Rehabilitative Services. Accessed at www.ed.gov /inits/commissionsboards/whspecialeducation/reports/info.html on January 21, 2011.

Ravitch, D. (2010a). *The death and life of the great American school system: How testing and choice are undermining education.* New York: Basic Books.

Ravitch, D. (2010a). Leading educational scholar Diane Ravitch: No child left behind has left US schools with a legacy of "institutionalized fraud." *Democracy Now.* Accessed at www.democracynow.org /2010/3/5/protests on December 12, 2010.

Rebora, A. (2010). Responding to RTI. *Education Week Teacher PD Sourcebook, 3*(2), 20. Accessed at www.edweek.org/tsb/articles /2010/04/12/02allington.h03.html on January 21, 2011.

Reeves, D. (2011). *Finding your leadership focus: Transforming professional learning into student results, K–12.* Thousand Oaks, CA: Corwin Press.

Renkl, A., Atkinson, R., Maier, U., & Staley, R. (2002). From example study to problem solving: Smooth transitions help learning. *Journal of Experimental Education, 70,* 293–315.

Rivkin, S. G., Hanushek, E. A., & Kain, J. F. (2005). Teachers, schools, and academic achievement. *Econometrica, 73*(2), 417–458. Accessed at http://edpro.stanford.edu/Hanushek/files_det.asp?FileId=73 on January 21, 2011.

Robinson, V. M. J. (2007). *School leadership and student outcomes: Identifying what works and why.* New South Wales, Australia: Australian Council for Educational Leaders.

Rogers, E. (2003). *Diffusion of innovation* (5th ed.). New York: Free Press.

Rosenshine, B., Meister, C., & Chapman, S. (1996). Teaching students to generate questions: A review of the intervention studies. *Review of Educational Research, 66,* 181–221.

Ross, D., Bondy, E., Gallingane, C., & Hambacher, E. (2008). Promoting academic engagement through insistence: Being a warm demander. *Childhood Education, 84*(3), 142.

Sagor, R. (1992). *How to conduct collaborative action research.* Alexandria, VA: Association for Supervision and Curriculum Development.

Saphier, J. (2005). *John Adams' promise: How to have good schools for all our children, not just for some.* Acton, MA: Research for Better Teaching.

Saphier, J., King, M., & D'Auria, J. (2006). 3 strands form strong school culture. *Journal of Staff Development, 27*(3), 51–59.

Schlechty, P. (2005). *Creating the capacity to support innovation* [Occasional Paper No. 2]. Louisville, KY: Schlechty Center. Accessed at www.schlechtycenter.org/tools-for-change on January 10, 2010.

Schmoker, M. (2006). *Results now: How we can achieve unprecedented improvement in teaching and learning.* Alexandria, VA: Association for Supervision and Curriculum Development.

Sergiovanni, T. (2005). *Strengthening the heartbeat: Leading and learning together in schools.* San Francisco: Jossey-Bass.

Shulman, L. (1983). Autonomy and obligation: The remote control of teaching. In L. S. Shulman and G. Sykes (Eds.), *Handbook of teaching and policy.* New York: Longman.

Sparks, D. (1984). Staff development and school improvement: An interview with Ernest Boyer. *Journal of Staff Development, 5*(2), 32–39.

Stevenson, H. W., & Stigler, J. W. (1992). *The learning gap: Why our schools are failing and what we can learn from Japanese and Chinese education.* New York: Simon & Schuster.

Stigler, J. W., & Hiebert, J. (1999). *The teaching gap: Best ideas from the world's teachers for improving education in the classroom.* New York: Free Press.

Stigler, J., & Hiebert, J. (2009). Closing the teaching gap. *Phi Delta Kappan, 91*(3), 32–37.

Strong American Schools. (2008). *Diploma to nowhere.* Washington, DC: Author.

Swanson, C. B. (2009, June 11). Gauging graduation, pinpointing progress. *Education Week.* Accessed at www.edweek.org/ew/articles /2009/06/11/34progress.h28.html?intc=ml on January 21, 2011.

Taylor, K., & Rohrer, D. (2010). The effects of interleaved practice. *Applied Cognitive Psychology, 24,* 837–848.

Teach for America. (2010). *Our mission and approach.* Accessed at www .teachforamerica.org/mission/mission_and_approach.htm on May 20, 2010.

Teaching Commission. (2004). *Teaching at risk: A call to action.* New York: Teaching Center. Accessed at www.csl.usf.edu/teaching%20 at%20risk.pdf on December 20, 2010.

Teaching Commission. (2006). *Teaching at risk: Progress and potholes.* Washington, DC: Author.

Tichy, N. (1997). *The leadership engine: How winning companies build leaders at every level.* New York: Harper Business.

Timperley, H., & Alton-Lee, A. (2008). Reframing teacher professional learning: An alternative policy approach to strengthening valued outcomes for diverse learners. *Review of Research in Education, 32,* 328–369.

Tyack, D., & Cuban, L. (1995). *Tinkering toward Utopia: A century of public school reform.* Boston: Harvard University Press.

Tyler, R. W. (1949a). *Basic principles of curriculum and instruction.* Chicago: University of Chicago Press.

Tyler, R. W. (1949b). *Constructing achievement tests.* Chicago: University of Chicago Press.

United States Census Bureau. (2009). *Table A-3: Mean earnings of workers 18 years and over, by educational attainment, race, Hispanic origin, and sex—1975 to 2008* [Data file]. Accessed at www.census.gov /hhes/socdemo/education/data/cps/historical/index.html on February 25, 2011.

United States Census Bureau. (2010). *A half-century of learning: Historical census statistics on educational attainment in the United States, 1940 to 2000—Table 1* [Data file]. Accessed at www.census.gov /hhes/socdemo/education/data/census/half-century/introduction .html on February 25, 2011.

Weisberg, D., Sexton, S., Mulhern, J., & Keeling, D. (2009). *The widget effect: Our national failure to acknowledge and act on differences in teacher effectiveness.* Brooklyn, NY: New Teacher Project. Accessed at http://widgeteffect.org/downloads/thewidgeteffect_execsummary .pdf on January 21, 2011.

WestEd. (2000). *Teachers who learn, kids who achieve: A look at schools with model professional development.* San Francisco: Author.

Whittier Union High School District. (2008). USC researchers confirm Whittier Union to be a "district of excellence" [Press release]. Accessed at www.wuhsd.k12.ca.us/whittieruhsd/usc_wuhsd_dist _excellence.pdf on August 19, 2009.

Witziers, B., Bosker, R. J., & Kruger, M. L. (2003). Educational leadership and student achievement: The elusive search for an association. *Educational Administration Quarterly, 39*(3), 398–425.

Wright, S., Horn, S., & Sanders, W. (1997). Teacher and classroom context effects on student achievement: Implications for teacher evaluation. *Journal of Personnel Evaluation in Education, 11,* 57–67.

Index

Raising the Bar and Closing the Gap: Whatever It Takes
Richard DuFour, Rebecca DuFour, Robert Eaker, and Gayle Karhanek
This sequel to the best-selling *Whatever It Takes: How Professional Learning Communities Respond When Kids Don't Learn* expands on original ideas and presses further with new insights. **BKF378**

Revisiting Professional Learning Communities at Work™: New Insights for Improving Schools
Richard DuFour, Rebecca DuFour, and Robert Eaker
This 10th-anniversary sequel to *Professional Learning Communities at Work™* offers advanced insights on deep implementation, the commitment/consensus issue, and the human side of PLC. **BKF252**

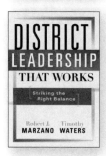

District Leadership That Works: Striking the Right Balance
Robert J. Marzano and Timothy Waters
Learn strategies for creating district-defined goals while giving building-level staff the stylistic freedom to respond quickly and effectively to student failure. **BKF314**

The Highly Engaged Classroom
By Robert J. Marzano and Debra J. Pickering
With Tammy Heflebower
Key research and practical strategies enable all teachers to create a classroom environment where engagement is the norm, not the exception. **BKL005**

a division of

Solution Tree | Press
Solution Tree

Visit solution-tree.com or call 800.733.6786 to order.